EARLY CHRISTIAN SYMBOLISM
IN GT. BRITAIN AND IRELAND:

THE ROMANO-BRITISH PERIOD
AND CELTIC MONUMENTS
WITH AN ACCOUNT OF
EARLY CHRISTIAN SYMBOLISM
IN FOREIGN COUNTRIES

EARLY CHRISTIAN SYMBOLISM
IN GT. BRITAIN AND IRELAND:

THE ROMANO-BRITISH PERIOD
AND CELTIC MONUMENTS
WITH AN ACCOUNT OF
EARLY CHRISTIAN SYMBOLISM
IN FOREIGN COUNTRIES

BY J. ROMILLY ALLEN
being two of the
Rhind Lectures in Archaeology
for 1885

A FACSIMILE REPRINT
BY LLANERCH PUBLISHERS, 1992.
ISBN 0947992 95 2.

First published by Whiting & Co., London, 1887.

# CONTENTS

| | |
|---|---|
| Early Christian symbolism in foreign countries | 1-70 |
| Romano-British period and Celtic monuments | 71-129 |
| General Index | 130 |
| Index of subjects occurring in Christian art | 132 |
| Index of places | 135 |
| List of illustrations | 138 |

# LECTURE I.

## EARLY CHRISTIAN SYMBOLISM IN FOREIGN COUNTRIES

PREVIOUS TO ITS INTRODUCTION INTO GREAT BRITAIN.

THE subject chosen for the present course of lectures is Early Christian Symbolism, with special reference to its manifestations in Great Britain and Ireland. It is necessary at the commencement to define the exact meaning of the terms employed in the title. The word early has reference to the period of Christian art to be dealt with, and includes the space of five hundred years between the seventh and twelfth centuries. It will be seen, subsequently, that the amount of material for arriving at the history of Christian art in this country before the seventh century is very small indeed; and therefore our knowledge of the subject in the preceding period is derived almost entirely from foreign sources. I have fixed the year 1200 as the final limit of our investigation as regards time, because, in the thirteenth century an entire change took place in Christian art, which then ceased to be Byzantine in character and became mediæval; or, in other words, Northern influence began to predominate over Eastern. Symbolism may be defined as a means of conveying ideas and facts to the mind by representations, which are, in the first instance, merely pictorial, but by frequent repetition gradually assume certain stereotyped forms. It is, in fact, a conventional system whereby pictures of historical scenes or natural objects are made use of to express something beyond what appears to the eye; and set in motion a train of thought, leading the mind on to contemplate those abstract ideas that are associated directly, or otherwise, with the thing portrayed. For instance, the scene which shows Noah in the Ark, is pictorially merely a man in a boat; but symbolically is intended to teach the doctrine that, as God saved Noah from destruction in the waters of the flood, so will Christ deliver those who believe in Him from spiritual danger. Not only are the representations of events which actually took place, found in Christian art, but scenes from the mystical or supernatural portions of the Bible, such as the Apocalypse, are also of frequent occurrence. The subjects adopted for the purpose of Christian symbolism may be classified, either according to the nature of the event or thing by which the idea is suggested, or according to the book or tradition whence the knowledge of the event having taken place is derived. All symbolism in the first instance results from the contemplation of the surrounding universe; but with the development of abstract methods of thought, and the accumulation of ideas which results from the existence of literature, we obtain fresh sources of inspiration.

We have, then, the following classification of subjects, according to nature of the outward forms, suggesting the idea involved in the symbolism.

(1.) Historical Scenes, that is to say, events which are recorded as having actually taken place in this world, and are used as having a secondary meaning; as, for example, the Sacrifice of Isaac, which typifies the Crucifixion of our Lord.

(2.) Parables, or supposed events, which are already used in a secondary sense and, therefore, are allegorical in literature before being adopted in art, such as the Parable of the Wise and Foolish Virgins.

(3.) Mystical or Supernatural Scenes, connected with another world, such as the Dream of Ezekiel, or the Last Judgment.

(4.) Representations of Religious Rites and Ceremonies; the Church, and its officers.

(5.) Subjects symbolical of the Moral and Spiritual Life; such as the Soul, Death, the Christian Life, the Conflict between Good and Evil, the contrasts between Virtues and Vices, Deeds of Goodness and Deadly Sins.

(6.) Subjects suggested by the properties of the Animal, Vegetable, and Mineral World; such as the habits and qualities of birds, beasts, fishes, and minerals, which can be applied in a spiritual sense to Christian doctrines.

(7.) Subjects connected with the Universe and the operations of Nature—such as the Seasons, the Months, the Signs of the Zodiac, and the Sun, Moon, Stars, Earth, Wind, Rivers, etc., personified.

(8.) Human pursuits and occupations capable of being applied figuratively to the teaching of Christianity; as the trade of a fisherman, which is compared in the New Testament to that of a preacher of the Gospel.

(9.) Representations of inanimate objects occupying a prominent position in some historical scene, or associated with a particular idea; as, for example, the Cross and the Keys of St. Peter.

(10.) Monograms or symbols founded on combinations of letters.

The other method of classification to be considered, is where the subjects are arranged according to the sources in literature or tradition whence they are obtained, as follows:

(1.) Subjects founded on Pagan history, science or mythology, and adapted to Christian purposes; as, for instance, the Story of Orpheus applied to Christ.

(2.) Scriptural subjects, which are chiefly the Three Persons of the Trinity; Heaven and the Angels; Hell, the Devil and his Angels; scenes and persons described in the Old Testament typical of those in the New; and scenes and persons from the New Testament, specially chosen as having reference to the leading doctrines of Christianity.

(3.) Apocryphal subjects, derived from the uncanonical books of Scripture, such as the story of Susanna and the Elders, and the Harrowing of Hell; being generally only an amplification of the Bible narrative, filling in the details which are there omitted.

(4.) Subjects from the Lives of Saints, which, however, are rare in early Christian art.

(5.) Subjects founded on mediæval science, applied in a spiritual sense; as, for example, in the Bestiaries.

Systems of symbolism have existed in the most remote ages, long before the dawn of Christianity; as is shown by the fact that the phonetic alphabets of the Phœnicians, Greeks, and Romans were originally developed out of the primitive picture-writing or hieroglyphics of the Egyptians. Christian symbolism will consequently be found in its earlier stages to contain some of the elements of the pagan symbolism which preceded it. As centuries rolled on, Christian nations progressed in civilisation, and their ideas on spiritual matters underwent various modifications, so that the symbolism, which was the outcome of these ideas, changed also. In studying development, whether it be of plants or animals, or of ideas, no fact is more curious than the way in which archaic types survive, side by side with those which are the growth of yesterday. Thus some symbols have become extinct; others so profoundly modified as to be scarcely recognisable; whilst not a few remain to the present day absolutely unchanged in any respect from what they were a thousand years ago. For instance, the conventional representation of Adam and Eve is the same now as it was in the third century; whereas that of the Crucifixion has been materially altered. The reason of this is that, in the former case, no change of belief is involved, but in the latter new ways of considering the subject were introduced from time to time. At different periods of the Church's history, special portions of Scripture seem to have fired the imagination more than others, and particular dogmas were singled out to occupy a more prominent position; the result being at once apparent in the system of symbolism.

Survivals of archaic forms are due, not only to the more stable nature of particular doctrines, but also to the stereotyped modes of thought found in many of the nations who have embraced Christianity. This is specially noticeable in comparing the East with the West, for, although the Roman Church adapted its system of symbolism to suit new modes of thought, the religious pictures of the Greek Church are the same at the present day as those of the earliest times. Other survivals are owing to particular portions of the Christian Church having become isolated; as was the case with the Celtic Church during the Saxon invasion. Christian symbols may then be divided into three classes, namely:—

(1.) Those which have survived the destructive effects of time, and are in use in this country at the present time to express their original meaning.

(2.) Those which, although they have ceased to be used in this country, are to be found still in use abroad.

(3.) Those which have ceased to be used both in this country and elsewhere.

This latter class may again be subdivided into—

(a.) Those whose meaning is known either by inscriptions, or by written accounts, or by tradition.

(b.) Those whose meaning is quite unknown.

The scientific methods of archæology are applied to deciphering the meaning of Christian symbolic representations in the following manner. With regard to symbols belonging to the first class no investigation is necessary, as the original signification is still retained. The meaning of symbols belonging to the second class is ascertained by comparison with those still in use in other countries. Symbols belonging to the third class, which have gone out of use everywhere, must be arranged, and then compared with those whose meaning is known by inscriptions or history. There will, probably, always remain a large residue whose signification is entirely lost, and with regard to these, when the archæologist has classified and arranged them, his work is done. By this process the known is separated from the unknown, and should fresh discoveries be the means of explaining one symbol of a class, then all those which have been arranged with it will be understood as well; but, until new light is thrown upon some of them, we must be content to admit the limits of our knowledge, which is indeed the first step towards further progress. A great deal of harm has been done to archæology, and much discredit has been justly thrown on this pursuit, in consequence of the system of guesswork which has often taken the place of more scientific methods; and by the dislike of authorities on the subject to acknowledge, frankly, their inability to give explanations.

And in this matter the public must take no small share of the blame, for an explanation of some kind, although known to be grossly improbable, is always expected, and is preferred to the admission of ignorance. If the same careful methods that are applied to other branches of scientific research were used by the archæologist, equally valuable discoveries would be the result, but as long as a system of guesswork prevails there can be no hope of progress.

In some symbolic representations, the group of figures in the scene may be so dramatically arranged, and may correspond so exactly in every particular with the description given in the Bible of some striking incident, that the interpretation is not difficult. It must not, however, be forgotten that a confusion may arise from the partial resemblance of different scenes: as for example, the Transfiguration and Ascension of Christ.

In addition to the systems of symbolism already described, there is the purely arbitrary one, where a particular geometrical shape or graphical picture of some object is taken to represent an idea which has no connection with the thing itself, as for instance, the Greek letter $\pi$, which is used by mathematicians to express the ratio of the diameter of a circle to its circumference. Once the meaning of any of these arbitrary symbols is lost, there is no conceivable method of scientific comparison by which it can be recovered.

Any attempt at explaining mediæval symbolism from a nineteenth century point of view is certain to end in failure. All ideas which are the result of modern culture must be laid aside, and an endeavour must be made to imbue ourselves thoroughly with the spirit of the thinker of the Middle Ages, and try and see things as he saw them, remembering that political and religious changes have entirely altered the cast of the national mind, and that advances of knowledge have completely revolutionised science and art. For instance, everyone is now familiar with the appearance of foreign animals, from having seen either the beasts themselves in menageries, or illustrations of the various species in books on natural history. These sources of information were, however, quite unknown in the Middle Ages; and it is not, therefore, surprising to find the imagination supplying the place of actual knowledge in the wonderful stories told of lions, tigers, elephants and all kinds of fabulous beasts, or to observe the grotesque shapes they assume in ancient illuminations and sculpture. The mediæval naturalist did not dissect and classify animals scientifically, but he seems to have paid attention chiefly to such of their real or supposed habits and qualities, as would enable him to make religious capital out of the subject by appending morals to the description of each, in order to convey some spiritual lesson to the mind of the reader. Before the Reformation, science did not exist in the modern acceptation of the word, and all learning was turned into a religious channel.

The only possible way of understanding early Christian symbolism is to study mediæval literature, and by searching the contemporary manuscripts, find out what was the conventional method of treating particular scenes, and what the actual ideas were of the artists who drew them. The rudeness of the execution of some of the early Christian sculptures has proved a stumbling-block to many enquirers, who have misinterpreted the meaning of the subjects represented entirely, by not making sufficient allowance for the want of art-training existing in remote places and times. These sculptures, like the designs on ancient British coins, were copied from well-executed classic models, and are quite unintelligible until placed side by side with the originals, when the meaning is at once apparent. Many errors have arisen from the custom, common in remote districts far away from the centres of learning, of portraying figure-subjects in the dress of the day; in consequence of which, Scripture scenes have been sometimes mistaken for representations of contemporary events. The most usual dress for Scripture characters is, however, long flowing drapery, probably copied originally from the Roman costume, and handed down by means of miniatures in manuscripts from one century to another. It cannot be too clearly pointed out, that the system of early Christian symbolism was a general one, and dealt either with scenes from the Bible, which were intended to inculcate some vital truth, or with emblems typical of some special virtue which the Christian should possess, or vice that he should avoid, and not with the doings of public personages or private individuals, however celebrated. Portraits of some of the French emperors are found as frontispieces to MS. Bibles; and occasionally miniatures of Saints occur, as, for example, St. Jerome starting on his journey to revise the Scriptures, or St. Benedict promulgating his rule. These are rare exceptions, and the representation of a purely secular or historical event, having no connection with the Church, is probably not to be found on any Christian monument, or in any MS. of a religious book.

In order to understand the early Christian symbolism of Great Britain, it will be necessary to take a brief survey of the chief sources whence the materials for the study of Christian art, generally, are obtained. These are as follows:—

A.D. 50 to 400.—Paintings in the decoration of the walls and roofs of sepulchral chambers in the Catacombs at Rome. Sepulchral tablets ornamented with Christian symbols from the Catacombs. Sculptured sarcophagi from the Catacombs. Objects found in the Catacombs, such as gilded glass vessels, lamps, &c.

A.D. 400 to 700.—Paintings and mosaics in the decoration of the walls, roofs, and floors of ecclesiastical buildings in Italy and the East. Sculptured sarcophagi from the early basilicas at Rome, Ravenna, Milan, Marseilles, Arles, and elsewhere. Carved ivories, chiefly diptyches, caskets, etc. Miniatures in Greek and Syriac MSS., coins, engraved gems, etc. Holy oil-vessels.

A.D. 700 to 1050.—Paintings and mosaics in the decoration of the walls, roofs, and floors of ecclesiastical buildings in Italy and the East. Pre-Norman sculptured crosses in Great Britain. Miniatures in Greek, Carlovingian, Lombardic, and Celtic MSS. Carved ivories. Belt clasps from Burgundian graves.

A.D. 1050 to 1200.—Decorative features of ecclesiastical buildings in Europe, such as paintings and mosaics on walls and roofs; mosaic, marble, tile or other pavements; doors ornamented with metal-work or wood-carving; stained glass windows; sculptured architectural details of columns, capitals, arches, etc. Ecclesiastical fittings of churches, such as altars, pulpits, fonts, screens, etc. Ecclesiastical furniture and utensils, such as shrines, croziers, vestments, chalices, crucifixes, etc. Miniatures in English, French, German, Spanish, and other MSS. Carved ivories. Sepulchral monuments.

It will be noticed that almost all the sources enumerated in the above list are connected either with the rites of religion or burial; and that at different periods the materials for the study of Christian art have to be sought in a new geographical area, and on a special set of objects. There are various causes which have co-operated to produce this result. During the era of the persecution of the Christian Church by the Roman emperors, between the years A.D. 64 and A.D. 303, religious art is entirely confined to the underground cemeteries which were purposely made inaccessible by means of concealed entrances and other precautionary measures.

The open use of Christian symbols elsewhere, would doubtless have been speedily followed by a martyr's death.

In the year 312 peace was restored to the Church, and Christianity thenceforward became the religion of the state, so that, there being no further need for secrecy, basilicas soon sprang up in all directions. The most appropriate method of decorating the large masses of wall-surface and the domed roofs of these early churches was either with frescoes or mosaic; the latter being chosen in preference during the 500 years between the fourth and ninth centuries. Most of the sculptured sarcophagi belong to 200 years (A.D. 350 to 550), during which the burials took place in the cemeteries round the suburban basilicas, above ground, before the time of intramural interments. The reason that sculptured sarcophagi were not employed to any great extent before the middle of the fourth century is, that during the time of persecution, the moving of such heavy masses of stone would have attracted attention to the entrances of the Catacombs, which it was desirable from motives of safety to conceal. The art of the sculptor was also a dangerous one for a Christian to pursue, as he was forbidden by the Church to make pagan idols, and his refusal to do so would compel him to confess his faith at the risk of his life. The use of sculptured sarcophagi ceased when other forms of sepulchral monuments were introduced.

From the eighth to the eleventh centuries, the mosaic decorations of churches still is the chief form in which Christian art exhibited itself in Italy; but by this time the religion had spread over a far larger area than was the case previously, and the examples of early symbolism in Great Britain must be sought in the Celtic and Saxon MSS. and sculptured stones, as it was on these that the highest skill of the workman was lavished. The ecclesiastical buildings were then of the plainest description, and have almost all been destroyed. During this period the same kind of contest was going on in Great Britain between Christianity and paganism as was the case in Rome during the first three centuries. In the eleventh and twelfth centuries the Danish and Saxon wars ceased, and after the Norman Conquest the Church became firmly established. As it grew rich its buildings became more important, and, consequently, the materials for studying the history of Christian art are much more numerous than before. Sculpture became a leading feature in the decoration of churches, wall-paintings were largely used, and encaustic tile pavements, and stained glass windows, introduced for the first time. Ecclesiastical vestments, and all objects appertaining to the church were ornamented with Christian symbols and figure-subjects. The MSS. are also more numerous, and illustrated by a greater number of miniatures. At this time, however, symbolism ceases to be found to any great extent on sepulchral monuments, which consist either of recumbent effigies or slabs with plain crosses upon them. The large doors of some of the churches and Cathedrals abroad ornamented with symbolic sculptures and metal-work, belong to this period.

Ivory carvings with Christian subjects are found from the fourth century onwards, and will be referred to hereafter.

Having now reviewed the sources whence the materials for the study of early Christian symbolism are obtained, and having considered the changes which have taken place during each successive century in the localities where they are to be sought, and the structures or objects on which they are found, the next point to be dealt with is the quality of the art exhibited. That of the paintings in the Catacombs and on the earlier sculptured sarcophagi during the first four centuries, is debased Roman or classical art. The result of Greek art reacting upon Roman art, when the seat of government was removed to Constantinople, in A.D. 328, was to produce the Byzantine style which is seen in the mosaics of the Italian basilicas, and has survived to the present day in the paintings of the Greek Church.

From the time of Charlemagne, A.D. 742, when the Northern nations were incorporated in Christendom, Teutonic and Lombardic art began to react upon Byzantine art, the result being the production of the Carlovingian, or what may be called the Northern-Byzantine style. Celtic and Spanish early Christian art also owe their origin to the Byzantine style, but each have their peculiar characteristics, which will be referred to hereafter. Gradually, the Northern element became predominant, and, in the thirteenth century, the Northern-Byzantine style developed into the Gothic or mediæval. The present course of lectures deals only with that period when the influence of Byzantine art continued to be felt in Great Britain, and which terminates in about the year A.D. 1200.

Since early Christian symbolism in this country traces its origin, first to Byzantium, and then to Rome, it is absolutely essential to know something of subjects treated in the paintings in the Catacombs, on the sculptures of the Sarcophagi, on the mosaics in the Basilicas, and, in fact, on all those works of Christian art previous to the eighth century. The remainder of this lecture will therefore be devoted to acquiring that knowledge of the growth of Christian symbolism in its birthplace, which is to form the basis of subsequent investigation.

## The Catacombs at Rome.

The derivation of the word Catacomb has not been satisfactorily settled. The underground burial-places of the early Christians in Rome were originally called cemeteries, or places of repose. When the knowledge of the existence of the principal cemeteries was lost during the thirteenth and fourteenth centuries, one still remained open beneath the Basilica of St. Sebastian, on the Via Appia, which was called in all the ancient documents, "Cœmeterium ad Catacumbas"; and the name Catacomb was in the course of time given to all similar subterranean burial-places.[1]

There are about sixty different localities where catacombs occur, all situated in the suburbs of Rome, near the principal highways, within a radius from one to three miles of the wall of Servius Tullius[2]; and their extent may be gathered from the statement of De Rossi that, if stretched out in one continuous

---

[1] Northcote and Brownlow's *Roma Sotterranea*, vol. i, p. 262.

[2] The catacombs are placed at a distance from the city on account of the Roman law forbidding burial within the walls.

line, the total length of the passages would exceed 350 miles. The position chosen is invariably on high ground, so as to avoid the possibility of the excavations being flooded with water, and the geological formation is volcanic tufa, which is dry, easy to work, and not liable to fall in, so that it is suited in every way for the purpose required. The Catacombs consist of a series of galleries, ranging from 2 to 4 ft. wide, and seldom exceeding 10 ft. in height, cut in the solid rock, with passages branching out at right angles, and leading in many cases into square chambers or "cubicula" with domed roofs. The galleries always preserve a horizontal direction, and there are often as many as three tiers one above the other, access being gained from one to the other by means of steps, but never by a sloping descent. The entrances to the oldest Catacombs, such as that of Domitilla, were doorways of classical style of architecture situated near the public highway. During the period of persecution, it became necessary to conceal the openings by various devices. Access is now obtained to the Catacombs either from the churches erected over their sites, after the persecutions had ceased, or from the vineyards in the neighbourhood of Rome.

The simplest form of grave in the Catacombs is called a "loculus", and consists of a rectangular recess, cut horizontally in the side of the walls of the passages and chambers, large enough to contain one or more dead bodies. The *loculi* are ranged in tiers one above the other like the berths in a ship, and are closed by a slab of marble or terra-cotta, flush with the surface of the wall, upon which is incised or painted the epitaph of the deceased, together with certain Christian symbols having reference to a future life. The more important graves are called "arcosolia", and are formed by first cutting an arched recess horizontally in the side wall, and then hollowing out a sarcophagus vertically beneath it to contain one or more corpses.

The vaulted roofs of the chambers and the arches of the "arcosolia" were plastered and ornamented with paintings of figure-subjects, having reference to the doctrines of Christianity. The lighting and ventilation of the chambers were effected by means of vertical shafts leading to the surface of the ground, called "luminaria".

The cemeteries took their names first from the private individuals who owned the ground where the burials were made, but afterwards from the Martyrs who were buried there. Thus the cemetery of Domitilla is, in later times, known as that of SS. Nereus and Achilleus.

The Catacombs were not old quarries or sandpits, as has been suggested, but were purposely excavated as burial-places. This is clear from the fact that the rock in which the galleries are cut is unsuitable for building purposes, and the sandpits are made much broader, so as to facilitate the removal of the soil. The workmen who made the Catacombs were called "fossors", and their appearance, and the nature of the implements they used, may be gathered from the well-known picture of "Diogenes Fossor" in the cemetery of Domitilla, of the fourth century; where he is shown wearing a loose tunic, and having a pick over his shoulder and a lamp in his hand. At his feet lie an axe and a hammer, and the pair of compasses with which he set out his work. The rectangular plots of ground belonging to individuals, which formed the sites of the earlier cemeteries, were small, perhaps measuring about 200 ft. by 100 ft., and situated at the side of a road. The method of construction was to make an entrance by a flight of steps down to the proper depth at one corner, and then strike out two galleries at right angles to the extreme extent of the area occupied, to serve as base-lines for further operations. Finally, the whole space was filled in with a network of galleries opening into chambers at intervals.

After the year 202, the cemeteries ceased to be the property of private individuals, and were transferred to the guardianship of the community of Christians as a body corporate, who appointed a special officer to administer them. Consequently, the smaller private cemeteries were gradually absorbed in larger ones, much in the same way that a city, when it extends, swallows up all the surrounding villages. In later times, the ground plan of the passages became still further modified on account of the crowding of burials round particular spots, caused by the desire to be near the tomb of some particular Saint or Martyr. When burials ceased in the Catacombs, in the year 410, the alterations which took place were chiefly with a view of rendering the different shrines more accessible and convenient for pilgrims, by closing up passages in which they might get lost, and making larger openings to let in light.

The chief evidence as to the history and age of the catacombs is obtained from coins, tiles bearing stamped names and inscriptions with the names of Roman Consuls found *in situ*. Valuable information as to the names of the different cemeteries, and the martyrs buried in them, has been derived from the study of the ancient martyrologies, the itineraries or guide-books for the use of pilgrims, some of which are as old as the fourth century, the "Liber Pontificalis", the Christian Almanack of Furius Dionysius Filoculus (A.D. 354), and the Monza Papyrus (A.D. 600).[1]

The history of the Catacombs may be divided into five periods.

(1) A.D. 50 to 410.—The period of burial, during the last 210 years of which the cemeteries ceased to belong to individuals and became the public property of the Church.

(2) A.D. 350 to 850.—The period of pilgrimage, during the first 200 years of which burials took place in the suburban cemeteries above ground, and afterwards within the walls of Rome.

(3) A.D. 650 to 850.—The period of the removal of the relics.

(4) A.D. 850 to 1578.—The period of abandonment.

(5) A.D. 1578 to 1886.—The period of modern research.

*First Century.*—The evidence as to the antiquity of cemeteries belonging to the first century, rests entirely for proof on the traditions contained in the ancient itineraries and martyrologies, and the character of the formulæ and names in the inscriptions. Only one dated inscription of the first century has been found in the Catacombs, and is now in the Lateran Museum. It is of the third year of Vespasian, or A.D. 71, a mere fragment, containing nothing more than the date; and, unfortunately, the locality whence it came is unknown.[2] According to De Rossi, there are at least five cemeteries as old as the first century; namely, the crypts of the Vatican, the traditional burial-place

---

[1] Northcote and Brownlow, vol. i, chap. II.
[2] Northcote and Brownlow's *Epitaphs of the Catacombs*, p. 29.

of St. Peter; and that of St. Paul's extra-muros, where the body of the Apostle of the Gentiles is supposed to rest; the cemeteries of Priscilla, on the Via Salaria Nova; of Domitilla on the Via Ardeatina; and the Cœmeterium Ostrianum, on the Via Nomentana.

*The Second Century.*—Two inscriptions only of the second century have been found in the Catacombs, both in the crypt of St. Paul's extra-muros. One is scratched on the mortar round a grave, and contains the names of the Consuls Sura and Senecio (A.D. 107). The other is on marble, and records the names of the Consuls Piso et Bolanus (A.D. 110).[1] Four cemeteries are attributed by De Rossi to the second century, on the ground that, according to the old calendars and martyrologies, the festivals of martyrs who perished at that time were held at their tombs in the catacombs. The four cemeteries referred to are; that of St. Hermes, on the Via Salaria, whose martyrdom took place not later than the reign of Hadrian (A.D. 117-120); that of Maximus, on the Via Salaria Nova, in which was held the festival of SS. Filicitas and Silanus, martyred A.D. 162; that of the Jordani, on the Via Salaria Nova, in which was held the festival of SS. Vitalis and Martial, martyred A.D. 162; and that of Pretextatus, on the Via Appia, containing the tomb of S. Januarius (martyred A.D. 162), and the inscription erected to his memory by Pope Damasus (A.D. 366-385).

*The Third Century.*—The cemeteries ceased to belong to private individuals after the year A.D. 202, when Pope Zephyrinus (A.D. 192-215) set the deacon Callixtus over the cemetery (*i.e.*, that called after his name on the Via Appia). In the crypt of St. Eusebius, in the cemetery of Callixtus, an inscription to the effect that "The Deacon Severus made this double chamber, with its *arcolosia* and *luminare*, as a quiet resting-place in death for himself and his relatives, by permission of his Pope Marcellinus" (A.D. 296-308). It is in the third century that the regular series of historical inscriptions begins; the earliest being one now in the Lateran Museum, belonging to the year A.D. 238. There are about thirty other dated inscriptions between this and the year 300. In the Papal Crypt in the cemetery of Callixtus have been found the epitaphs of five Popes, namely, Urban (A.D. 230),

[1] Northcote and Brownlow's *Roma Sotterranea*, vol. i, p. 114.

Anteros (A.D. 235), Fabian (A.D. 236-248), Lucius (A.D. 251), St. Eutychianus (A.D. 258). In the year A.D. 257 the first imperial edict against the Catacombs being visited or used as places of assembly was issued by Decius. The third century is the era of persecution, when the entrances to the Catacombs were purposely concealed and the passages blocked up so as to render them inaccessible.

*The Fourth Century.*—At the beginning of the fourth century the persecutions of the Christians ceased, and, in the year 312, peace was restored to the Church by the Edict of Milan. A new era in the history of the Catacombs was thus inaugurated, and Christianity became the religion of the state, so that, there being no further necessity for concealment, Basilicas began to be built above ground, round which the burials took place, instead of in the subterranean galleries. During the latter half of this century interments in the Catacombs became less and less frequent, and, after the year A.D. 371, the subterranean burials almost entirely ceased. The earliest dated inscription found in the cemeteries of the suburban basilicas above ground belongs to the year A.D. 358. When the Catacombs were no longer used as burial places the tombs of saints and martyrs still continued to be visited by large numbers of pilgrims. Pope Damasus (A.D. 366-385) altered the Catacombs so as to adapt those portions where the bones of the martyrs lay for use as shrines. He blocked up passages where pilgrims might get lost, made access to the tombs to be visited easier and more direct, improved the lighting and ventilation, and finally wrote commemorative verses which were inscribed on marble tablets in each of the sacred localities.

*The Fifth Century.*—After the capture of Rome by Alaric (A.D. 410) there were no more burials in the Catacombs, except in the special case of the bodies of bishops and martyrs brought from abroad, and none of any kind whatsoever took place after A.D. 450. All mention of the fossors ceases after A.D. 426.

*The Sixth Century.*—In A.D. 537 the tombs of the martyrs were injured by the irruption of Vitiages, but they were subsequently restored by Pope Virgilius (A.D. 538-555). After the devastation of Rome by Totila (A.D. 560-574), burial without the walls was rendered unsafe on account of the disturbed state of the surrounding country, and the latest dated inscription found in the suburban cemeteries above ground belongs to the year A.D. 565. After this all burials took place within the walls of Rome; masses, however, still continued to be held in the Catacombs every Sunday, by order of Pope John III (A.D. 560-574).

*The Seventh Century.*—In the year A.D. 648 the translation of the relics of saints from the Catacombs to the Basilicas within the walls was commenced by Pope Theodore and continued by Pope Leo II (A.D. 682), but masses were still held in the subterranean chambers by the order of Pope Sergius (A.D. 687).

*The Eighth Century.*—In consequence of the devastations and sacrileges committed by the Lombards under Astolphus (A.D. 756), Pope Paul I removed the relics of more than one hundred saints from the Catacombs, and the natalia only of martyrs were celebrated, by order of Pope Gregory III (A.D. 731).

*The Ninth Century.*—In the year A.D. 817, 2,300 bodies were removed from the Catacombs to Sta. Prassede by Pope Paschal I, but no translations of relics are recorded after the days of Pope Leo IV (A.D. 848). In the year A.D. 860 Pope Nicholas I visited the cemeteries and restored in some of them the celebration of mass, which had ceased for many ages previously.

*The Tenth to the Thirteenth Century.*—During the next four hundred years only occasional visits to about five cemeteries are recorded.

*The Fourteenth Century.*—At this time only three cemeteries attached to suburban churches were known, namely those of SS. Hermes, Valentine, and Saturninus.

*The Fifteenth Century.*—At the beginning of the fifteenth century only one cemetery remained open, namely, that known as the "Cemeterium ad Catacumbas", beneath the church of St. Sebastian, on the Via Appia. It is recorded that, between the years A.D. 1432 and 1482, the Catacomb of St. Callixtus was visited by Franciscan Friars, some Scotchmen, and Roman academicians, none of whom, however, understood the meaning of what they saw.

*The Sixteenth Century.*—The Catacombs were rediscovered in the year A.D. 1578 by some workmen, who accidentally broke into a gallery of graves, ornamented with Christian paintings, whilst digging for pozzolana in a vineyard on the Via Salaria.

Although this discovery excited universal attention at the time it was made, no real investigations were set on foot until Antonio Bosio's first visit to the Catacombs, in A.D. 1593, at the age of eighteen. Between this time and his death he spent a period of thirty-six years in the most indefatigable examination of about thirty cemeteries, the result of which was given to the world in his *Roma Sotterranea*.

*The Seventeenth Century.*—In the year A.D. 1629 Antonio Bosio died, but his *Roma Sotterranea* was not published until three years afterwards (A.D. 1632-1635). All further investigations in this century, until A.D. 1668, were made by private individuals, who kept no record of what was found, and the scientific results of their discoveries are therefore irretrievably lost. In A.D. 1651 P. Aringhi brought out a Latin translation of Bosio's work with considerable alterations and omissions. In A.D. 1688 Pope Clement IX put a stop to private explorations, and appointed a custodian over the Catacombs.

*The Eighteenth Century.*—In the year A.D. 1700 R. Fabretti, the official custodian of the Catacombs, explored and described two new Catacombs, which were unknown to Bosio. M. A. Boldetti succeeded Fabretti as custodian, and the result of the discoveries during more than thirty years in which he held the office were published by him in A.D. 1720. Buonarroti, Boldetti's assistant, wrote a work, in 1720, on the gilded glass vessels found in the Catacombs. In A.D. 1737, Bottari republished Bosio's plates by the command of Pope Clement XII. Seroux d'Agincourt visited the Catacombs (A.D. 1780-1786) to collect materials for his history of the decline of the fine arts. The Christian Museum at the Vatican was founded by Pope Benedict XIV, in A.D. 1756, and it contains many objects of great interest from the Catacombs.

*The Nineteenth Century.*—In 1841 Padre Marchi, the custodian of the Catacombs, commenced those investigations which have since been continued by Giovanni Battista de Rossi with such extraordinary success. De Rossi's researches are the only ones which have been made on a scientific principle; and the results he has arrived at are of the utmost possible value to archæology and throw a flood of new light on the history of early Christian symbolism. The Christian Museum in the Lateran, containing inscriptions from the Catacombs and sarcophagi, was founded by Pope Pius IX in A.D. 1854.[1]

Having concluded the historical description of the Catacombs, the next points to be considered are the art and symbolism of the paintings on the walls and roofs of the chambers. The art as exhibited during the first four centuries, whilst burials still took place in the Catacombs, is debased Roman art, differing but little in its earlier stages from the classical designs found in Pompeii, and not shewing any marked change until it was merged in the Byzantine style in the fifth century. The ornamental features consist of wreaths of flowers, scrolls of vines and foliage, and sometimes birds and animals. The designs are always disposed symmetrically, and surrounded by margins. The figures are tolerably well proportioned, generally having flowing drapery, except in the case of Adam and Eve, Jonah, and Daniel, who are shown naked. The head-dresses worn fit close to the head and are of classical shape,[2] but the heads are generally shown without any covering, and having short curling hair. A marked peculiarity is the entire absence of the nimbus round the head. The feet are shod with sandals in most cases. Christ is universally represented as being of youthful appearance, with a pleasing countenance and destitute of beard.

The symbolism of the paintings in the Catacombs, as has been previously remarked, shows a considerable admixture of Pagan ideas, and this may be partly accounted for by the necessity for disguising Christian doctrines during the times of persecution under forms that would not be easily recognised, and partly because it is almost impossible to create a new system of symbolism without founding it to a certain extent on what has gone before. The most distinctly Pagan subject adopted by the Christians, but with a new signification, was that of Orpheus

[1] During the times of persecution some of the larger chambers in the Catacombs were possibly used as places of assembly and for religious worship, but this does not affect the symbolism of the paintings in any way.

[2] The Three Magi, and the Three Children in the Fiery Furnace, wear Phrygian caps, and the Jews have a special cap.

charming the beasts with the sound of his lyre, which occurs in three places in the Catacombs. The best instance is in the cemetery of Domitilla, where this subject is associated with others of a distinctly Christian nature, such as the raising of Lazarus.[1] The application of the story of Orpheus to Christian doctrines is, that as Orpheus allured the beast by the sound of his lyre, so are sinners drawn towards Christ by the teaching of the Gospel. The representation of our Lord as the Good Shepherd has also been traced to a Pagan origin, from the resemblance to such statues as that of Hermes-Kriophorus.[2] However, both in this case and that of Orpheus, there is a marked difference between the copy and the original, for the Christian figures are always clothed, whereas the Pagan ones are undraped. The painting of the four seasons, of which there is an example in the cemetery of Pretextatus, perhaps as old as the second century,[3] is a subject which may be equally Christian or Pagan. Personifications of earth, river-gods, figures of Sol and Luna, etc., were also borrowed from classical sources, but generally in later times than those of the Catacombs.

After the system of Christian symbolism founded on Pagan originals, but with a new meaning, come a series of scenes from the Old Testament which are used as types of those in the New; the most common being:—

(1.) The Temptation of Adam and Eve; typifying the necessity of a Saviour to wash away the effects of the fall of man with His blood.

(2.) Noah in the Ark; where the ark symbolises the Church of Christ, by means of which believers may be saved from the destruction of the surrounding world.

(3.) Abraham's sacrifice of Isaac; which typifies the sacrifice of Christ for the sins of the world.

(4.) Moses striking water from the Rock; typifying Christ the spiritual rock and source of living water.

(5.) Moses putting off his shoes at the Burning Bush; where Moses, being chosen by God to deliver the children of Israel from the bondage of the Egyptians, foreshadows Christ's delivery of believers from the bondage of sin.

---

[1] Northcote and Brownlow's *Roma Sotterranea*, vol. ii, p. 31.
[2] *Ibid.*, p. 28.   [3] *Ibid.*, p. 149.

(6.) Daniel in the Lion's Den.
(7.) The Three Children in the Fiery Furnace.
(8.) Jonah (four scenes—(*a*) swallowed by the whale; (*b*) thrown up by the whale; (*c*) under the shadow of the gourd; (*d*) the gourd withered).

The last three, Nos. 6, 7, and 8, show forth God's promise to deliver the true believer from danger, and the story of Jonah also has reference to the Resurrection of Christ after the third day.

David with his sling occurs in one rare instance.[1]

The scenes from the New Testament, chosen for preference by the artists who decorated the chambers of the Catacombs, are those which refer to the doctrines of the Resurrection, the Eucharist, and the healing by faith, the ones which occur most frequently being as follows:—

(1.) The Raising of Lazarus, foreshadowing the Resurrection of Christ.

(2.) The Miracle of the Loaves and Fishes.

(3.) The Miracle of Changing the Water into Wine.

(4.) The Feast of the Seven Disciples by the Sea of Tiberias; all three having reference to the Eucharist.

(5.) The Miracle of Healing the Blind, showing the power of Christianity to open the eyes of the soul.

(6.) The Paralytic carrying his bed.

(7.) St. Peter saved from drowning; both examples of the power of faith.

Other subjects, which are found less frequently, are the Virgin and Child, the Adoration of the Magi, Herod and the Magi, the Baptism of Christ, the Parable of the Wise and Foolish Virgins, and Christ with the Woman of Samaria.

In the paintings of the Catacombs, besides scriptural scenes, the first germs appear of that elaborate system of symbolism, founded upon the real or supposed qualities and habits of birds, beasts, and fishes, which received its highest development in the mediæval bestiaries. The ideas of which this system are the outcome, have been partly derived from the Bible, and partly from the books on natural history of the ancients, such as that of Pliny, and from the fabulous tales told of particular beasts. The

---

[1] Northcote and Brownlow, vol. ii, p. 31.

animal which is most frequently seen in the paintings of the Catacombs is the sheep, either being carried on the shoulders of the Good Shepherd, or forming portion of the surrounding pastoral scene. The sheep symbolise the members of the flock of Christ. The most remarkable instance of this class of symbolism is in the Catacomb of St. Callixtus, where Susannah and the elders are shown as a lamb between two wolves.[1] There is no doubt as to the meaning of the picture, for over the lamb, which has bells round its neck, is inscribed the name SVSANNA, whilst above one of the wolves on each side is written SENIORIS (*i.e.*, seniores). The scene recalls our Lord's words, " Behold, I send you as lambs amongst wolves." The two birds which occur most frequently are the dove and the peacock. The dove, which in many cases has an olive branch in its mouth, either represents the soul of the departed, or refers to the message of peace, telling of a haven of rest which was brought to Noah in the Ark. In the scene of the Baptism of Christ the Holy Spirit appears as a dove. The peacock is supposed to be a type of the Resurrection, on account of the legend that its flesh is incorruptible, and that it sheds its feathers in the winter only to attire itself in plumage of more brilliant hue in the spring. Opinions differ as to the interpretation of the dolphin, which is used as a symbol in the Catacombs often associated with the anchor. The fish generally is used as a type of Christ, because of the acrostic quoted by Eusebius and St. Augustine, in which the Greek word for fish forms the first letters of the Greek words for " Jesus Christ, the son of God, Saviour."[2] Other symbols are taken from the vegetable creation; as, for instance, the vine, which Christ, in His own words, has made a type of Himself. The occupations of everyday life is the source whence the symbols of the ship, the anchor, and the wine jar are taken. The ship has a double meaning, and is taken either, like the Ark of Noah, to represent the Church in which Christians are carried safely through the perils of this world, or to symbolize the prosperous ending of a voyage when the soul enters its haven of rest. Sometimes, the dove with the olive branch, the messenger of peace, appears on the prow, and the mast takes the form of the

[1] Northcote and Brownlow's *Roma Sotterranea*, vol. ii, p. 171.
[2] *Ibid.*, p. 61.

cross. The anchor, which occurs so often in association with the dolphin, signifies, in the words of St. Paul, "hope, the anchor of the soul, both sure and steadfast." The amphora, or wine-jar, stands for the soul, the word being used in Scripture to mean an instrument chosen by God.

In addition to the subjects already described there are others which deserve notice. The intervention of the Almighty in the scene of Moses and the Burning Bush is expressed by a hand emerging from a cloud,[1] and in the case of a shipwreck the head and arm are shown as well.[2] In a large number of the paintings isolated figures, both male and female, occur, known as "oranti", with the hands out-stretched in the ancient attitude of prayer; but the various authorities differ as to the explanation whether the Church, the Virgin Mary, or a private individual is intended to be represented.[3] A man, standing beside a well, is to be found in some of the paintings, and the interpretation which has been suggested is that it is the well whence spiritual waters are to be drawn for the refreshment of believers.[4]

The palm-branch is a symbol taken from the Pagan custom of giving it as the reward of victory, and is used to express the triumph of those who have conquered in the fight, or won the race of life.

There are several examples of people seated at a feast, the symbolism of which has not been satisfactorily explained.[5] The representations of the Fossors, who excavated the Catacombs, have been previously referred to. The earliest example of the Chi Rho monogram of Constantine, which occurs engraved on an inscribed tombstone in the Catacombs, belongs to the year A.D. 331, and, in conjunction with the Alpha and Omega, it is not found until A.D. 362.[6] There are only two instances of the monogram of Constantine occurring in paintings in the Catacombs of St. Callixtus at the end of the fourth century.[7] Some of the paintings in which the nimbus is introduced round the heads of the figures may possibly be as old as the end of the

[1] Northcote and Brownlow's *Roma Sotterranea*, vol. ii, p. 180.
[2] *Ibid.*, p. 154.   [3] *Ibid.*, p. 137.   [4] *Ibid.*, p. 101.
[5] Northcote and Brownlow, vol. ii, p. 124.
[6] Northcote and Brownlow's *Inscriptions*, p. 30.
[7] Northcote and Brownlow, vol. ii, p. 183.

fourth century, but its use was not by any means common until a much later date.¹

There are two classes of symbols not distinctly Christian in character, which are found on the tombstones in the Catacombs; (1) representations of implements used in particular trades, to show the occupation followed by the deceased; and (2) pictorial rebuses or puns on the names of the person buried, as a ship (*navis*) against the epitaph of Nabiva, and a pig against that of Porcella. In the preceding description of the symbolism of the Catacombs the subjects which are engraved or painted on the tombstones have been included with those of the paintings on the walls and roofs of the chambers, but there are some symbols, such as the anchor, the wine-jar, and the ship, which are almost entirely confined to the tombstones.

The domed roofs of the chambers present the surface best adapted for decoration by means of frescoes, and the subjects are generally arranged symmetrically with definite relation to each other. One example from the cemetery of St. Marcellinus will give an idea of the rest.² In the centre is the Good Shepherd, and in eight surrounding compartments, divided geometrically, are two scenes from life of Jonah, Daniel in the Lion's Den, Moses striking the Rock, Noah in the Ark, the Paralytic carrying his bed, the Miracle of the Loaves and Fishes, the Raising of Lazarus.

Next to the domes of the chambers, the ancosolia were most suitable for forming centres round which to group paintings; the semicircular recessed space at the back, the soffit of the arch above the grave, and the portions of the wall of the chamber at each side and below the arch being all made use of. A favourite arrangement was to have the Good Shepherd in the middle, and Moses striking the Rock placed in contrast with the Raising of Lazarus on each side.

The essential characteristic of the paintings in the Catacombs is that they are symbolical and not historical, the subjects chosen being always those which lend themselves most easily to the former method of treatment. In the earlier examples the groups consist of as few figures as possible, only the leading

¹ Northcote and Brownlow's *Roma Sotterranea*, vol. ii, p. 190.
² Garrucci, *Storia del Arte Cristiana*, vol. ii, p. 51.

actors in some specially dramatic scene are shown, without any accessories which would detract from its simplicity, or draw away the attention from the central action. Thus the Good Shepherd stands alone, bearing the lost sheep on his shoulder. Daniel is a single naked figure, with hands outstretched in the ancient attitude of prayer, between two lions placed symmetrically on either side. Noah is placed in an actual box (*arca*), and from this fact only, and from the dove being shown flying towards him, is the meaning made clear. Moses with an uplifted wand in his hand pointed towards a rock from which gushes forth a stream of water, constitutes a whole scene; and, lastly, Christ appears in a similar attitude, calling forth Lazarus from the tomb, a small building like a sentry-box, with the upraised corpse, still swathed in its grave bandages, standing in the doorway. Subsequent developments in symbolical representations consisted in adding to the number of actors in the scenes, and making the surroundings more elaborate; but it must not be forgotten that the object involved in these changes was not to carry the symbolism into the minute details, but merely to make the picture more complete. The original germs of the later compositions are generally to be found in the earlier catacomb paintings, which served as models for all that came after. Another point to be noticed is that as symbolism was the main object of the paintings the artist did not look upon historical accuracy as by any means necessary; thus, in the miracle of the loaves and fishes, the specified number of baskets' full of fragments is varied, and in the story of Jonah the fish is not a whale, but a conventional sea monster.

In dealing with Christian art abroad, my object is not so much to give an exhaustive account of its various phases, as to point out the general nature of the sources whence the symbolism of this country originated, and to show what facilities exist at home for studying the subject more fully, should anyone wish to do so.

The materials available in this country for becoming acquainted with foreign archæology consist of objects obtained from abroad, and now deposited in museums; reproductions by means of casts or photography; and, lastly, illustrations and descriptions in books. The principal museums are the British

Museum, containing a collection of the highest possible interest, but badly arranged and uncatalogued; the South Kensington Museum, which has an admirable reference library connected with it, and a series of handbooks and catalogues, leaving little to be desired. The National Museum of Scotch Antiquities, and the Edinburgh Industrial Museum, are the best establishments of the kind in Scotland; and the Museum of the Royal Irish Academy, in Dublin, contains a unique collection of Celtic works of art. Throughout the country there are many local museums, but very few of any importance, except those of Liverpool, Sheffield, York, Newcastle, and Salisbury. With regard to information derived from books I think it is a mistake merely to give a list of authorities, as is generally done, without saying anything as to their relative merits, or as to the contents and illustrations. Writers may be divided into two distinct classes, those who make original researches, and those who compile treatises from the works of others.

Original research is often found buried in the transactions of learned societies, or published in volumes so large and expensive as to be quite beyond the reach of the general public, hence the necessity of the compiler, or book maker, to put the information together and present it in a palatable form to the ordinary reader. The value of the work of the book-maker depends entirely upon the skill with which he digests the materials at his disposal, and the critical acumen he displays in separating the wheat from the chaff. Anyone who wishes to study a subject thoroughly must eventually refer to the original authorities, but, in order to get a general idea of its scope, he should begin by reading a compilation. I shall endeavour, therefore, in describing the various sources of the materials for the study of Christian Symbolism, to point out (1) the best compilation or text book on each subject; (2) the original authorities; (3) the most accurate illustrations; (4) the reproductions or objects brought from abroad existing in our museums.

With regard to the paintings in the Catacombs, the most complete and reliable account is to be found in Northcote and Brownlow's *Roma Sotterranea*, compiled from the works of De Rossi; Bourgon's *Letters from Rome;* Maitland's *Church in the Catacombs;* and Wharton Marriott's *Testimony of the Catacombs*, may also be read with advantage.

The original works on the Catacombs are A. Bosio's *Roma Sotterranea* (A.D. 1632), a translation of which was published by Aringhi (1651), and the plates reproduced by Bottari (1737); Boldetti's *Osservazioni supra i cimeteri dei SS. Martini ed antichi Cristiani di Roma* (1720); and, most important of all, G. B. de Rossi's *Roma Sotterranea* (1664), containing accurate descriptions of researches made under the author's supervision, chiefly in the cemetery of Callixtus. For illustrations, consult Bosio's *Roma Sotterranea*, and Garrucci's *Storia del arte Cristiana*, vol. ii. A series of photographs of the paintings in the Catacombs have been published by the late J. H. Parker.

### GILDED GLASS VESSELS FROM THE CATACOMBS
### (A.D. 250-350).

Of all the objects which have been found in the Catacombs, the most interesting to the student of Christian archæology are certain fragments of gilded glass vessels with figure subjects and inscriptions. The number of specimens known to exist is about 340,[1] the greater part of which are preserved in the Vatican Library at Rome, the remainder being in the museums in London, Paris, Florence, and Naples. With the exception of two fragments found at Cologne, the whole of these have been discovered in the cemeteries near Rome, generally sticking to the plaster of the "loculi". In most cases all that remains is the bottom of the vessel, which being stronger than the rest, has survived, whilst the thin edges have perished. A nearly perfect example is figured by Garrucci,[2] from which it appears that the shape was that of a shallow bowl or patera, having in the centre a circular medallion with a figure subject upon it, executed in the following manner: the artist took a round piece of glass and, having fixed a leaf of gold upon it with some kind of cement, traced the design with a sharp-pointed instrument, afterwards attaching the whole to the bottom of the vessel by fusion produced by heat. Sometimes silver leaf and colour were

---

[1] The rarity of these objects may possibly be accounted for by their having been destroyed for the sake of extracting the gold.
[2] Copied in Martigny's *Dict.*, art. "Fonds de Coupe," p. 328.

used. Most of the gilded glass vessels have inscriptions of two kinds: (1) explanatory of the subject represented; and (2) of a convivial character, showing that they were used for drinking purposes. As example of the latter we have the following:—

DIGNITAS AMICORVM PIE ZESES CVM TVIS OMNIBVS VIVAS,

"A mark of friendship, drink, and long life to thee and all thine."

The words PIE ZESES for the Greek πίε ζήσῃς, or "Drink, and long life to you", are of very frequent occurrence. It has not been satisfactorily settled on what occasions these cups were used.

Northcote and Brownlow[1] suggest that they were connected with the celebration of the feast of SS. Peter and Paul, whose figures are found on eighty of the 340 specimens known. Martigny[2] thinks some may have been sacramental, and others for the *agapes*—(1) at a funeral feast, when the subjects refer to Resurrection, (2) at a wedding feast, when the ceremony of marriage is represented, (3) natal feasts, when children are shown, (4) the festivals of Saints whose portraits appear on the vessels.

De Rossi assigns the gilded glass from the Catacombs to a period ranging from the middle of the third to the beginning of the fourth century. One fragment bears the name of Marcellinus, who was martyred under Diocletian A.D. 304.[3] No specimens have yet been found in any of the cemeteries or churches above ground, which became common after A.D. 312.

Although the number of representations of Christian subjects on the gilded glass vessels is small as compared with those derived from other sources, yet the amount of light they throw on early symbolism is out of proportion with their numerical quantity, on account of the existence of so many inscriptions explaining the meaning of the figures, and thus supplying a key to the interpretation of similar ones in the Catacomb paintings, and on the sculptured sarcophagi. The most elaborately ornamented glass vessels are those which have a central subject surrounded

---

[1] *Roma Sotterranea*, vol. ii, p. 308.
[2] *Dict. des ant. Chrét.*, p. 328.
[3] Garrucci, p. 32, No. 5.

by others arranged in a circle outside; then there are ones with a central subject only, enclosed in a circular medallion; and, lastly, there are vessels decorated with a large number of much smaller medallions, scattered over the whole surface of the plate. As an example of the first kind we may take one belonging to Mr. Wilshere. In the centre is the portrait of a man and his wife, with the inscription "PIE ZESES", "Drink and long life to thee!" surrounded by the following scenes from Scripture.

(1) The Temptation of Adam and Eve.
(2) The Sacrifice of Isaac.
(3) Moses striking the Rock.
(4) The Paralytic carrying his Bed.
(5) The Raising of Lazarus.

It will be noticed that the symbolism and the arrangement of the subjects is exactly the same as that found on the paintings of the circular domes of the chambers in the Catacombs, except that on the glass vessels we have a secular representation in the centre, instead of the figure of the Good Shepherd or some scene from Scripture. Another vessel of the same class in Mr. Wilshere's Collection has St. Peter and St. Paul in the centre, surrounded by six radial compartments, containing:

(1) The Three Children in the Fiery Furnace.
(2) A man standing in front of a symbolic figure of the Sun, which is supposed to refer to the text in Isaiah (lx, 20).[1]
(3) A woman in the ancient attitude of Prayer.
(4) The Prophet Isaiah being sawn in two (Heb. xi, 37).
(5) Moses and the Brazen Serpent.
(6) Moses striking the Rock.

The gilded glass vessels are particularly interesting, as affording us a large number of inscribed portraits of our Lord, the Virgin Mary, the Apostles, and Saints, both male and female. Our Lord is shown young and beardless, as in the Catacomb paintings, and without the nimbus, except in one rare instance. The name is written either CRISTVS, or ZESVS CRISTVS, and the Saviour appears sometimes alone, or between St. Peter and St. Paul, or seated on a throne with saints at each side, or raising Lazarus. Our Lord also appears as the Good Shepherd. The legend above the head of the Virgin is MARIA, and she is

---

[1] Martigny's *Dict.*, art. "Prophètes", p. 684.

placed, in an attitude of prayer, between St. Peter and St. Paul, or between two doves. Of the apostles, St. Peter and St. Paul occur more frequently than any others, either alone, or with Christ, or a crown, or the Chi Rho monogram, or the Virgin Mary between them. In the Vatican Library at Rome there is a large circular medallion from the bottom of a glass vessel,[1] the scene on which resembles very closely that found on the mosaic decoration of the apse of the church of SS. Cosmas and Damian, at Rome (A.D. 526-530).[2] The picture is divided into two parts by a horizontal line. In the upper compartment our Lord is represented standing on an elevation, holding a scroll in his hand, inscribed (DOM)INVS, with St. Peter bearing the cross on his left, and St. Paul on his right. On each side are palm trees, the one behind St. Paul having a bird, with the nimbus round the head, perched in the branches. From inscribed examples, which occur on a leaden seal of the deacon Siriacus, and over the doorway of the ancient Basilica of St. Paul,[3] we know this bird to be the Phœnix, the symbol of the Resurrection. The legend round the glass vessel is PIE ZE(SES). The scene shown in the lower compartment is the Lamb of God standing on Mount Zion (Rev. xiv, 1), from which flow the four rivers of Paradise, symbolising the Four Evangelists, and uniting in the mystic Jordan, the name of which is inscribed IORDANES. On the right is the city of Bethlehem (BECLE), and on the left, Jerusalem (IERVSALE), from the gates of each of which three sheep are issuing, to symbolise the Jews and the Gentiles.[4]

We have also on the glass vessel portraits of the Apostles Timothy, Simon, Luke, and Judas; of male Saints, Hippolytus, Lawrence, Vincent, Callixtus, Marcellinus, Ciprianus, Sixtus Justus, Florus, etc., and of female Saints, Agnes, Peregrina, Libernica, Anne, etc. Of the scripture scenes from the Old Testament, perhaps the most remarkable is the Apostle Peter striking the rock instead of Moses, as is shown by the name PETRVS, which is inscribed above the head of the figure holding

---

[1] Northcote and Brownlow's *Roma Sotterranea*, vol. ii, p. 317.
[2] Parker's *Mosaics of Rome and Ravenna*, p. 19.
[3] Martigny's *Dict.*, art. "Phénix", p. 641.
[4] The same thing occurs on the mosaics at Sta. Maria Maggiore, SS. Cosmas and Damian, and St. Mark.

the rod. Upon the engraved glass plate found at Podgoritza, in Albania, a similar representation occurs, inscribed, "Petrus virga perquod set, fontis ciperunt quorere", for "Petrus virga percussit, fontes cæperunt currere", or "Peter strikes the rock, streams begin to flow."

The other Old Testament subjects are the same as those of the paintings in the Catacombs, and are as follows:—The Temptation of Adam and Eve, Noah in the Ark, the Sacrifice of Isaac, Moses striking the Rock, Moses and the Brazen Serpent, the Spies carrying the Bunch of Grapes, Daniel in the Lion's Den, Jonah and the Whale, Jonah under the Gourd.

The scenes from the New Testament are:—The Miracles of the Loaves, the Miracle of Cana, the Paralytic carrying his bed, the Raising of Lazarus.

The scenes from the Apocrypha are:—Tobit and the Fish,[1] Daniel giving the balls of pitch to the Dragon.

In addition to the above, we have the ceremony of marriage shown by a male and female figure grasping each other's hands over an altar above which is a crown, the legend being VIVATIS IN DEO.[2] Jewish symbols also occur, such as the seven-branched candlestick; the ark containing the rolls of the law[3]; domestic scenes, such as parents and children together; secular occupations, such as the chase, carpentry, coining money, driving chariots, etc.; and scenes from pagan mythology, such as Hercules, Achilles, gods and goddesses.

Besides glass vessels ornamented with gilding we have those where the design is produced by engraving, of which the most interesting specimen is a plate found at Podgoritza,[4] the ancient Doclea, in Dalmatia. It is 9¼ inches in diameter, and bears the following scenes and inscriptions, by means of which we are enabled to identify similar representations in the Catacomb

---

[1] Martigny's *Dict.,* art. "Tobie", p. 760.

[2] Northcote and Brownlow's *Roma Sotterranea*, vol. ii, p. 303; and Martigny's *Dict.*, art. "Mariage Chrétien", p. 446.

[3] Martigny's *Dict.*, articles "Évangiles", p. 298, and "Candélabre des Juifs", p. 113.

[4] Northcote and Brownlow, vol. ii, p. 318; engraved in Garrucci, *Storia del Arte Cristiana*.

paintings: In the centre, uninscribed—The Sacrifice of Isaac. Round the circumference—

(1) The Temptation of Adam and Eve, ABRAM ET FI EVAM.

(2) Raising of Lazarus, DOM(I)NVS LAZARVM.

(3) Moses-Peter striking the Rock, PETRVS VIRGA PERQVOD— SET FONTIS CIPERVNT QVORERE.

(4) Daniel in the Lion's Den, DANIEL DE LACO LEONIS.

(5) The Three Children in the Fiery Furnace, TRIS PVERI DE EGNE CAMI(NO).

(6) Susanna, in attitude of prayer, SVSANA, DE FALSO CRIMINE.

(7) Jonah in the boat, being swallowed by the whale, and under the gourd, DIVNAN DE VENTRE QVETI LIBERATVS EST.

With regard to the facilities for studying the gilded glass vessels from the Catacombs available in this country, we have in the British Museum a very good representative series, comprising many specimens of high interest. Mr. Wilshere also possesses a good private collection.

All the 340 known examples have been engraved by Garrucci, in his *Storia del Arte Cristiana*, but twenty are lost, and have been copied from Buonarotti's *Osservazioni sopra alcuni frammenti di vasa antichi di vetro, ornati di figure trovate nè di cimitiri di Roma* (Florence, 1716), who has described and illustrated seventy of them. The chapter on the subject in Northcote and Brownlow's *Roma Sotterranea*, and the article in Montigny's *Dictionnaire des Antiquités Chrétiennes*, and Dr. Smith's *Dictionary of Christian Antiquities*, will supply all the information necessary for obtaining a knowledge of the nature of the symbolism.

### SCULPTURED SARCOPHAGI (A.D. 250-650.)

The practice of enclosing dead bodies in sarcophagi, or receptacles formed out of solid blocks of stone, can be traced back to the time of the Egyptian kings who built the great pyramids. The Christians seem to have adopted this common Pagan method of burial in the earliest cemeteries, such as that of Domitilla, belonging to the first or second century; but during the persecutions the use of sarcophagi was abandoned owing to the danger of exposure which would follow from moving about the large masses of stone requisite, and from Christian symbols being publicly seen in the sculptor's workshop. The sarcophagi were placed in arched recesses in the sides of chambers prepared specially for their reception, or in the grand corridors, or on the landings of the staircases. During the second and third centuries the sarcophagi gave place to rectangular hollows cut in the solid rock, of which the sides of the chambers in the Catacombs were composed, instead of in blocks of stone provided for the purpose. These rock-cut sarcophagi are called *arcosolia*, and differ from the ordinary graves, or *loculi*, in being excavated vertically downwards beneath an arch, instead of horizontally in the sides of the passages. We learn from Northcote and Brownlow's *Roma Sotterranea*,[1] that "even when the Christians did bury their dead in sarcophagi, they do not appear, until the ages of persecution had passed away, to have ornamented them with sculptures of a distinctively Christian character. Out of 493 dated inscriptions, described by De Rossi as belonging to the first four centuries, only eighteen are found on sarcophagi, and not more than four bear dates anterior to the time of Constantine. These are ornamented with genii, or griffins, or pastoral or hunting scenes; and the earliest dated sarcophagus, with a distinctively Christian subject sculptured upon it, is one from the Catacomb of SS. Peter and Marcellinus, upon which is represented the Nativity, bearing a consular date ('Placido et Romulo'), corresponding to the year A.D. 343. . . . . . Since sculpture cannot be said to have existed as a Christian art before the time of Constantine, we may safely attribute nearly all the sarcophagi with distinctively Christian subjects sculptured upon them, to the fourth and fifth centuries. They come from the cemeteries above-ground, or from the basilicas and oratories erected in them."

At Urbino there is a very interesting tombstone of the third century, on which a Christian sarcophagus-maker, named Eutropus, is shown at work. The carving is being executed by means of a drill revolved by a cord wound round the spindle, and pulled backwards and forwards. The inscription is:

ΑΓΙΟC ΘΕΟCΕΒΕC ΕΤΤΡΟΠΟC ΕΝ ΙΡΗΝΗ

[1] Vol. ii, p. 235.

("Holy, God-fearing Eutropus in peace"), and at the right-hand corner is the dove with the olive-branch.

Sarcophagi may be divided into two classes : (1) those sculptured on one side only; (2) those sculptured on at least three faces, and generally on all four, and also on the top. The former are generally ornamented, partly with panels enclosing figures, and partly with panels covered with s-shaped grooves or wavy flutings, called "strigils", from their resemblance to the implement of that shape used by Roman gymnasts for cleaning the body. We have, as examples of this class, a sarcophagus, perhaps of the second century, from the crypt of Lucina,[1] inscribed BLASTIANE PAX TECVM, now in the Vatican; and another, still *in situ*, in the Catacomb of St. Callixtus,[2] with the Good Shepherd upon it. In the case of the sarcophagi sculptured on the back, front, ends, and top, the figures are arranged either in a single row, or in two tiers one above the other. Sometimes each group is placed under an arch or pediment, and separated from the next by a pillar, as is the case in the sculpture on Norman fonts. The sarcophagus of Junius Bassus[3] is a good example of this method of treatment. In most cases, however, all the groups representing the various scenes from Scripture are crowded together, as on the sarcophagus from St. Paul's extra Muros,[4] so that it is difficult to distinguish one from the other at first sight. Another plan of arrangement, which is also rather confusing, is to divide up the figures belonging to one scene into separate groups, by pillars placed at intervals, as on the sarcophagus of Anicius Probus.[5]

The composition of the design of the sculpture on one of the sarcophagi in the Lateran Museum[6] is quite exceptional and very clever. The principal feature of the whole is the story of Jonah, most graphically portrayed. In the centre are two sea-monsters, one swallowing the prophet, who is diving off the side of a vessel, and the other facing in the opposite direction towards the shore, and disgorging him. Above, on the shore, is the third scene, where Jonah is reclining under the

---

[1] Northcote and Brownlow, vol. ii, p. 238.
[2] *Ibid.*, p. 240.
[3] J. W. Appell's *Monuments of Early Christian Art*, p. 9.
[4] *Ibid.*, p. 16.    [5] *Ibid.*, p. 12.    [6] *Ibid.*, p. 19.

gourd. Every other available space which is left is filled in with groups of figures, so as to cover the entire surface, the most conspicuous being the Raising of Lazarus, Moses striking the Rock, Noah in the Ark, and a Man Fishing.

The art of the sculpture is, in the earlier examples, purely classical, getting more and more debased as time goes on, until, in the sixth and seventh centuries, it merges in the Byzantine style, which may be distinguished by the introduction of the nimbus round the heads of the figures, the lowness of the relief of the carving, and the figures being arranged more symmetrically in reference to a central group, and separated by wide intervals of plain background, instead of being closely packed together.

Far the most important collection of Christian sarcophagi is that in the Lateran Museum at Rome, commenced by Father Marchi in 1851, under the auspices of Pope Pius IX, and since completed by De Rossi. There are smaller collections in other places in Italy, chiefly at Ravenna, Pisa, and Milan. When Christianity spread to Gaul in the fourth and fifth centuries, the practice of burial in sarcophagi was introduced into that country, and a large number of them are now preserved in museums at Arles, Marseilles, and St. Maximin. In the chapel of Galla Placidia at Ravenna are three marble tombs of the fifth century, still in their original position,—(1) that of Galla Placidia (A.D. 440), now devoid of ornament; (2) that of Constantius III, her second husband (A.D. 421), and Valentinian, her son; (3) that of Honorius, her half-brother (A.D. 423). The subjects on the two last are, the Lamb; the two Doves on the Cross; the Drinking Doves; Palms; the Agnus Dei on Mount Zion, with the four Rivers. In the basilica of St. Vitale, at Ravenna, is the tomb of the Exarch Isaac (A.D. 644), with the Adoration of the Magi; and at the church of St. Apollinaris in Classe, in the same city, is a sarcophagus having a bas-relief of Christ, enthroned, with St. Peter carrying the cross on one side, and St. Paul on the other, and four Apostles, two of whom are carrying crowns of victory.

The most interesting sarcophagus as bearing on the question of early Christian symbolism is that of Junius Bassus, in the crypt of St. Peter's at Rome, because its date is fixed by unimpeachable historical evidence, and the series of sculptures with which it is adorned supply us with information as to the art of the fourth century, which it is impossible to obtain elsewhere. A classical cornice runs round the top, bearing the inscription: IVN . BASSVS VC QVI VIXIT ANNIS . XLII . MEN . II . IN IPSA PRÆFECTVRA VRBIS NEOFITVS IIT AD DEVM . VIII KAL SEPT EVSEBIO ET YPATIO COSS. ("Junius Bassus, who lived 42 years and two months. In the very year in which he was Prefect of the city he went to God, a neophyte, on the 23rd of August, Eusebius and Ypatius being Consuls.") This fixes the date as A.D. 359.

The sculptured figures on the front are arranged in two tiers, one above the other, each being divided into five groups by beautifully carved Corinthian columns. The subjects are as follows:

*Top Row.*—(1) The Sacrifice of Isaac; (2) Denial of Peter (?); (3) In the centre—Christ enthroned, with the personification of the heavens beneath His feet, and St. Peter and St. Paul on each side; (4) Christ before Pilate; (5) Pilate washing his hands.

*Bottom Row.*—(1) Sufferings of Job (?); (2) Temptation of Adam and Eve; (3) Christ's entry into Jerusalem; (4) Daniel in the Lions' Den; (5) Christ led away to Caiaphas (?), or the apprehension of Peter.

*In the Spandrels.*—The symbolic Lamb performing acts and miracles as follows: (1) The Three Children in the Furnace; (2) Moses striking the Rock; (3) Miracle of the Loaves; (4) Baptism of Christ; (5) Moses receiving the Law; (6) Raising of Lazarus.

The two ends of the sarcophagus are ornamented with representations of the Four Seasons, and the back is plain.

Amongst other sarcophagi in the Lateran Museum, the one from St. Paul's extra Muros (about fourth century) is specially deserving of notice, the subjects being as follows:—Creation of Eve; Fall of Adam and Eve; (in centre) Medallion, containing busts of a male and female; Miracle of Cana; Miracle of Loaves; Raising of Lazarus; Adoration of the Magi; Restoring sight to the Blind; Daniel in the Lions' Den (in centre); Habakkuk with loaves; Christ foretelling the Denial of Peter; the Apprehension of Peter; Moses striking the Rock.

Another example, possibly of the fifth century, is interesting as presenting the earliest known series of scenes from the Passion :—Christ bearing the Cross ; the Crowning with Thorns ; (in the centre) the Labarum of Constantine, with doves on each side, and two soldiers below ; Christ led before Pilate ; Pilate washing his hands.

There is also in the Lateran Museum a fine sculpture of the Ascent of Elijah, the idea of which is evidently taken from the chariot of the sun.

The following is a list of the subjects which occur upon the sculptured sarcophagi at Rome :[1]

God the Father—as a man creating Eve—as the Dextera Dei at the sacrifice of Isaac.

God the Son—as the Agnus Dei—as the Good Shepherd—as the Cross—enthroned between St. Peter and St. Paul—holding Cross, and standing on Mount Zion, with four rivers of Paradise.

The Apostles.

*Scenes from the Old Testament.*

Creation of Eve (12).
Temptation of Adam and Eve (14).
Adam and Eve condemned to work.
Offerings of Cain and Abel.
Noah in the Ark (5).
Sacrifice of Isaac (11).
Passage of the Red Sea.
Moses taking off his shoe (2).
Moses receiving the Law (4).
Moses striking the Rock (21).
Ascent of Elijah (2).
Vision of Ezekiel.
Three Children in the Furnace (4).
Daniel in the Lions' Den (14).
Habakkuk.
Daniel feeding the Dragon.
Story of Jonah (23).

[1] The numbers show the relative frequency with which the different subjects occur upon fifty-five sarcophagi in the Lateran Museum, and are taken from Burgon's *Letters from Rome.*

*Scenes from the New Testament.*

Nativity (1).
Adoration of the Magi (11).
Christ and Woman of Samaria.
Miracle of Cana (16).
Miracle of Loaves and Fishes (20).
Christ healing the Paralytic (12).
Christ healing the Blind (19).
Christ healing the Hæmorissa (8).
Christ raising Lazarus (16).
Christ raising Jairus's Daughter.
Entry into Jerusalem (6).
Denial of Peter (14).
Apprehension of Peter (20).
Christ before Pilate (5).
Christ crowned with Thorns (1).
Christ carrying the Cross (1).

On the sarcophagi of Gaul[1] we have the following additional subjects:—

*Scenes from the Old Testament.*

Fall of Quails in the Wilderness.
Fall of Manna in the Wilderness.
Two Spies carrying Bunch of Grapes.

*Scenes from the New Testament.*

Baptism of Christ.
Massacre of the Innocents.
Christ washing Disciples' Feet.
Betrayal.
Soldiers watching at the Sepulchre.
Delivery of Keys to St. Peter.
St. Peter raising Tabitha.
Martyrdom of St. Stephen.

Also we have the apocryphal story of Susanna and the Elders; the scene of the Passage of the Red Sea occurs far more frequently; the twelve Apostles are represented seated at

[1] See Martigny's *Dict.*, article "Sarcophages", p. 719; and Millin, *Midi de la France*—Atlas.

the feet of Christ, instead of standing; and the dolphin takes the place of the dove.

The art of the later Italian sarcophagi resembles that of the mosaics of the sixth century, and palm-trees, doves, peacocks, sheep, the nimbus, together with various forms of the Chi-Rho monogram, are introduced.

Inscriptions on sarcophagi explaining the sculptured subjects are very rare, but there is one instance at Saragossa, where the Fall of Adam and Eve has the legend, ADAN EVVA, the monogram over the head of Christ healing the Blind, and ISAC above the Sacrifice of Isaac, also ARON , INCRATIV PETRVS ET MARTA. In another case, from Spoleto, the Saviour and Four Evangelists are seen in a boat, inscribed IESVS , (IOH)ANNES , LVCAS , MARCVS.

A good general idea of the sculptured sarcophagi can be obtained from Dr. J. W. Appell's excellent little book, called *Monuments of Early Christian Art*, published by the South Kensington Museum authorities. The chapter in Northcote and Brownlow's *Roma Sotterranea* on the subject, and the article in Martigny's *Dictionary*, should also be read. The most complete and reliable series of illustrations is to be found in Garrucci's *Storia del Arte Cristiana*. Older engravings of those at Rome are given in Bosio's *Roma Sotterranea*, Bottari's *Sculture e pitture sagre*, etc. The ones in Gaul are illustrated in Millin's *Voyage dans les Départements du Midi de la France* —Atlas, and in Le Blant's *Inscriptions chrétiennes de la Gaule*.

Most of the sarcophagi at Rome have been photographed, either from the objects themselves or from casts, and the late J. H. Parker has published a series of them. I am not aware that there is a single cast of a Christian sarcophagus in any of our museums.

## Mosaics. (A.D. 350-850.)

The art of mosaic, or producing pictures suitable for the decoration of the walls and vaulted roofs of buildings, by means of an aggregation of small cubes of gilded or coloured glass, probably owes its origin to the tesselated pavements of the Romans. The latter were composed of pieces of marble of various hues, and the improvement introduced in mosaics during the early Christian period was to substitute artificial tesseræ for natural ones, and to make them of smaller and more even size, so as to be applicable to wall-surfaces instead of floors. Mosaic pavements were possibly derived from an Eastern source, and it is supposed by some that the "pavement of red, blue, and white and black marble", in the palace of King Ahasuerus, mentioned in the Book of Esther (ch. i, 6), was a work of this kind. Pliny describes a mosaic picture representing doves drinking out of a vase, executed by the artist Sosus for Attalus, King of Pergamus, about 200 B.C., which corresponds exactly with the mosaic now in the Capitoline Museum at Rome, known accordingly as "Pliny's Doves".

The Christian mosaics belonging to the first three centuries derived from the Catacombs are fragmentary in character and unimportant in number, but as soon as the first basilicas began to be built above-ground, the appropriateness of this method of decoration was at once recognised. All the finest mosaic pictures are to be found in the churches of Rome and Ravenna, although there are isolated examples at Constantinople, Mount Sinai, and elsewhere. The art-periods of the mosaics are as follows:—

A.D. 400 to 500 : Classical style.
A.D. 500 to 900 : Byzantine style.
A.D. 900 to 1100 : Decay of the art of mosaic; no examples extant.
After 1100 : Art of mosaic revived in style corresponding to that found in Western Europe generally.

The following are the principal specimens of mosaics belonging to the first, or Classical, period.

### Fourth Century.

A.D. 320.—Church of St. Constantia at Rome, a circular building surrounded by an aisle, the barrel vault of which is decorated with vintage scenes, foliage, birds, etc., but no distinctly Christian symbol. Ciampini preserves records of other mosaics of this period which have since disappeared. The mosaics of the Church of St. Agatha at Ravenna, built by Bishop Ursus, A.D. 378, have been lost. Constantine, in a letter to Maximus about the church at Constantinople, founded

A.D. 337, mentions the artists in mosaic who were employed there.

### Fifth Century.

A.D. 432-440.— Church of St. Maria Maggiore at Rome, decorated with mosaics executed in the time of Pope Sixtus III. On the walls of the nave, thirty pictures illustrating Old Testament history, chiefly taken from the lives of Abraham, Isaac, Jacob, Moses, and Joshua, arranged in double rows, one above the other, fifteen on each side. Some have been destroyed and others restored. On the east wall of the nave, above the arch of the tribune, scenes from the New Testament, in five rows,—the Annunciation, Presentation in the Temple, Jerusalem and Bethlehem, Lambs.

A.D. 461-467.—The oratory of St. John the Evangelist, in the baptistery of St. John Lateran, a square building, the vaulted roof of which is ornamented with mosaics executed for Pope Hilary, representing the Agnus Dei, surrounded by the symbols of the four Evangelists.

A.D. 440.—Church of St. Nazaro e Celso, or the Chapel of Galla Placidia, at Ravenna, a cruciform building, the domed roof of which is ornamented with mosaics, representing the Cross, surrounded by the symbols of the four Evangelists.

The chief mosaics in the Byzantine style are as follows:

### Sixth Century.

A.D. 526-530.—Church of SS. Cosmas and Damianus at Rome, built and decorated with mosaics by Pope Felix IV. On the east wall of the nave, above the arch of the tribune, the Agnus Dei, enthroned, surrounded by the seven lamps of fire which are the seven spirits of God, four angels, and the eagle of St. John and the angel of St. Matthew, as described in the Apocalypse (ch. iv). On the vaulted roof, forming a half-dome over the apse, a majestic figure of Christ in the centre, with a beard and nimbus, the right hand extended and the left holding a scroll. Below are a group of three figures on each side; on the right, St. Peter introducing St. Cosmas, who holds a crown in his hand, and behind him St. Theodore, also with a crown; on the left, St. Paul introducing St. Damianus, who has a crown in his hand, and behind him Pope Felix, holding a model of his church.

At the outside of each group is a palm-tree, the one on the left having the phœnix perched amongst its branches. Round the lower part of the domed roof runs a horizontal band of mosaic, representing the Agnus Dei, with the nimbus round the head, standing on Mount Zion, from the foot of which issue the four rivers of Paradise, uniting in one mystic Jordan. Six sheep on each side coming out of the gates of Jerusalem and Bethlehem, typify the Jews and the Gentiles.

A.D. 577-590.—Church of St. Laurence, without the walls of Rome, rebuilt and adorned by Pope Pelagius II, with mosaics on what was the east wall of the nave, above the arch of the tribune, representing Christ in the centre, seated on a globe and holding a cross; on the right, St. Paul, St. Stephen, and St. Hippolitus, holding a crown; on the left, St. Peter with cross, St. Laurence with cross, book, and model of church, and behind him Pope Pelagius II.

A.D. 547.—The Church of St. Vitalis at Ravenna is richly decorated with mosaics of the time of Justinian. On the vaulted roof of the apse, Christ seated on a globe, with an archangel on each side, the one on the right introducing St. Vitalis, to whom Christ is presenting a crown, and the one on the left introducing Ecclesius (Bishop of Ravenna, who died A.D. 541), the founder, carrying a model of his church. In the centre of the groined roof of the chancel, out of which the apse opens, the Agnus Dei, within a circular medallion. On the soffit of the chancel arch, in front of this vault, the heads of Christ, the twelve Apostles, Gervasius, and Protasius. On the jambs of the two side-windows of the apse, the four Evangelists with their symbols. On the north wall of the chancel, an historical group of eleven figures, including a portrait of the Emperor Justinian, preceded by Maximianus, Bishop of Ravenna, A.D. 547. On the south wall of the chancel, a similar group of ten figures, the principal one being the Empress Theodora. On the north wall of the choir above the altar, beneath a semicircular arch, the offerings of Abel and Melchisedec; on the right, the prophet Isaiah; on the left, Moses taking off his shoe; above the centre of the arch, two angels supporting a circular disc, on which is the cross and the Alpha and Omega; on the right, St. Mark and lion; on the left, St. Matthew and angel. On the south wall of the choir, above the altar, beneath a semicircular arch, Abraham entertaining the three men in the plains of Mamre (Gen. xviii), and the Sacrifice of Isaac. Over the crown of the arch, a pair of angels supporting the cross, as on the opposite side; on the right, Moses receiving commands from God; on the left, the prophet Jeremiah. Above, on the right, St. Luke and bull, and on the left, St. John and eagle.

A.D. 553.—The Arian baptistery, afterwards St. Maria in Cosmedin (or St. Mary the Beautiful), at Ravenna, is said to have been built by Theodoric, and has mosaics on its domed roof, representing the Baptism of Christ in the centre, surrounded by the twelve Apostles, six on each side of a throne, on which rests a jewelled cross.

The baptistery of St. John, in the cathedral at Ravenna, is said to have been built *circa* A.D. 451, but the mosaics are probably of the time of Bishop Maximian, who lived in the middle of the sixth century, and whose monogram is placed over one of the arches. The building is octagonal, and on the inside of the circular dome or cupola are mosaics representing the Baptism of Christ in the centre, with the figures of the twelve Apostles round it.

A.D. 567.—Church of St. Apollinare in Classe, near Ravenna, has mosaics on the domed roof of the apse, representing the Transfiguration, with St. Apollinaris below. On the east wall of the nave, above the arch of the tribune, Christ, the symbols of the four Evangelists, the Jewish and Gentile churches, symbolised by sheep issuing from Jerusalem and Bethlehem, and palm-trees. On the north wall of the nave, Archbishop Reparatus and the Emperor Constantinus Pogonotus. On the south wall of the nave, the sacrifices of the old Law, typified by the offerings of Abel, Melchisedec, and Abraham with Isaac.

A.D. 570.—Church of St. Apollinare Nuovo, built by Theodoric, and ornamented with mosaics on the north wall of the nave, representing the city of Classis (the port of Ravenna), with sea and ships in front, a procession of twenty-two female saints, headed by the three Magi, who are presenting their offerings to the Virgin enthroned with Child. Above are two rows of pictures; the lower one, figures of saints, and the upper one, thirteen scenes from the life of Christ, chiefly miracles. On the south wall of the nave the city of Ravenna, with a procession in front of twenty-five male saints, receiving the benediction from the Saviour, who is seated on a throne with an angel on each side. Above are two rows of pictures; the lower one, figures of saints, and the upper one, crowns suspended above the heads of each.

*Seventh Century.*

A.D. 626-638.—Church of St. Agnes, without the walls of Rome, built by Constantine, rebuilt by Pope Symmachus, and adorned by Pope Honorius with mosaics on the vaulted roof of the apse, representing the patron Saint Agnes in the centre, with Pope Honorius on the right, holding a book, and Pope Symmachus on the left, carrying a model of the church. Above the head of St. Agnes is a hand holding a crown.

A.D. 639-642.—Oratory of St. Venantius, near the baptistery of St. John Lateran at Rome, adorned with mosaics by Pope John IV. On the vaulted roof of the apse, busts of Christ in glory, giving the benediction, and an angel on each side; below, a group of figures, St. Mary in the centre, in the ancient attitude of prayer; on the right, St. Peter, St. John the Baptist, St. Domnius, and Pope Theodore; on the left, St. Paul, St. John the Evangelist, St. Venantius, and Pope John IV, carrying a model of the church. On the east wall of the nave, above the arch of the apse, the symbols of the four Evangelists, the two holy cities of Jerusalem and Bethlehem, and figures of Saints.

A.D. 642-649.—Church of St. Stephen, on the Cœlian Mount at Rome. On the vaulted roof of the apse, medallion bust of Christ, with hand holding crown above. Below, a large jewelled cross, with St. Felicianus on the right, and St. Primus on the left.

*Eighth Century.*

A.D. 796.—The Church of SS. Nereus and Achilleus, rebuilt by Pope Leo III, and ornamented with mosaics. On the east wall of the nave, above the arch of the apse, the Transfiguration. The mosaics of St. Pudentiana perhaps belong to this century, but there is so much doubt connected with their authenticity, that a description is omitted.

## Ninth Century.

A.D. 817-824.—Church of St. Maria, in Navicella, or in Dominica, rebuilt by Pope Paschal I, and ornamented with mosaics. On the vaulted roof of the apse, the Virgin and Child, enthroned, with Pope Paschal kneeling at her feet, and his monogram above her head; a crowd of saints on each side. On the east wall of the nave, above the arch of the apse, Christ in glory, within an oval aureole supported by two angels, and six Apostles on each side; in spandrels below, two figures of prophets.

A.D. 820.—Church of St. Prassede at Rome, rebuilt by Pope Paschal I, and adorned with mosaics. On the vaulted roof of the apse, a design similar to that in the Church of SS. Cosmas and Damian, a majestic figure of Christ standing in the centre; on the right, St. Peter, introducing St. Pudentiana, followed by St. Zeno, a palm-tree being behind; on the left, St. Paul introducing St. Prassede, followed by Pope Paschal, with the square nimbus, carrying a model of his church, a palm-tree being behind and the phœnix in its branches; below, a band with the Agnus Dei on Mount Zion, and the six sheep on each side, issuing from the gates of Jerusalem and Bethlehem. On the east wall of the chancel, above the arch of the apse, the Agnus Dei, enthroned, with the seven candlesticks, and symbols of the four Evangelists, illustrating the Apocalypse (ch. iv), copied, apparently, from the mosaics of SS. Cosmas and Damian; below, in the spandrels, the four-and-twenty Elders, with crowns. On the east wall of the nave, above the outer or chancel arch, Christ standing, with rows of saints and martyrs on each side. On the soffit of this arch, the monogram of Pope Paschal I (A.D 820).

A.D. 820.—The Church of St. Cecilia in Trastevere, beyond the Tiber, was built by Pope Paschal I, and adorned with mosaics. On the vaulted roof of the apse, Christ standing and giving the benediction, with a hand holding a crown above his head; on the right, St. Peter, St. Agatha, and St. Valerian; on the left, St. Paul, St. Cecilia, and Pope Paschal, carrying a model of the church; below, a frieze, with the Agnus Dei on Mount Zion, and the sheep issuing from the gates of Jerusalem and Bethlehem; at the top of the arch, the monogram of Pope Paschal I.

A.D. 858.—The Church of St. Maria Novæ Urbis, now St. Francesca Romana, at Rome, was rebuilt by Pope Leo IV, and adorned with mosaics. On the vaulted roof of the apse, the Virgin and Child, enthroned; on the right, SS. Peter and Andrew; on the left, SS. James and John; all under arcading, as on Norman fonts, etc.

This concludes the list of the most important examples of Christian mosaics at Rome and Ravenna up to the end of the ninth century, when the art fell into decay, and was not revived until a couple of hundred years later. In the twelfth century, when mosaics again make their appearance, the Byzantine influence was gradually declining, and the style of workmanship was assimilated to that generally prevalent in Western Europe.

The chief defect of most of the books which treat on mosaic decoration is, that plans of the buildings are not given side by side with the illustrations of the pictures on the walls and roofs, and it is therefore difficult to understand in what position many of the mosaics are placed. Under these circumstances, the reader is advised to consult the plans of churches given in Fergusson's *History of Architecture*, and the perspective views of the interiors to be found in Gally Knight's *Italy*. It will be seen there that the ecclesiastical buildings which are decorated with mosaics may be divided into two classes: (1) The basilicas, whose plan was derived from that of the Roman Halls of Justice, consisting of a rectangular nave and side aisles, with a semicircular apse at the east end; and (2) churches like St. Vitalis at Ravenna, and St. Sophia at Constantinople, whose architecture is akin to the domed structures found all over the East, with a more or less complicated ground-plan. In the cases of the basilicas, the chief surfaces suitable for decoration are as follows: (1) the roof of the apse in the form of a half-dome; (2) the east wall of the nave, above the arch of the apse and the spandrels on each side; (3) the north and south walls of the nave, in the space above the arcades, called in England the clerestory, but which is of large size, owing to the smallness of the arches below. The Eastern type of domed church presents a greater variety of surface for mosaics, on account of the nature of the ground-plan. The different surfaces may be thus classified according to shape: (1) Spherical surfaces, such as the domed roof of a round, square, or octagonal building, and the half-dome above a semicircular apse; (2) cylindrical surfaces, such as a barrel vault or the soffit of a semicircular arch; (3) flat surfaces of rectangular form, such as the north and south walls of the nave of a church; of semicircular form, such as the space under an arch or the tympanum of a doorway; of spandrel shape, at each side of a semicircular arch. With regard to the symbolism of the mosaics, the chief difference between those of classical style belonging to the fourth and fifth centuries, and the paintings of the Catacombs, is in the introduction of the symbols of the four Evangelists, the cross in place of the Chi-Rho monogram, and regular series of scenes from the Old Testament, arranged in historical order, instead of being classified according to their symbolism. At the Church of St. John Lateran, at Rome, we have an early example of the Agnus Dei, with the nimbus round the head, but without the cross.

The changes, however, which began in the sixth century, will be found to be of a far more sweeping character, and may be summed up shortly by saying that the art became essentially ecclesiastical, instead of Scriptural. The typical representation of Christ in the Catacomb paintings is as the Good Shepherd carrying back the lost sheep on His shoulders, youthful in appearance, and of a loving countenance; but on the mosaics of the sixth century, our Lord appears as a bearded man of advanced age, severe in aspect, and conveying the idea of Christ the Judge, rather than Christ the Saviour. The nimbus becomes common, being first placed round the head of the Agnus Dei and Christ in His human form, and afterwards applied to personages mentioned in the New Testament, and even to dignitaries of the Church. As the ecclesiastical element gradually began to predominate over the Scriptural, we find popes and patron saints, habited in regular vestments, carrying the models of their churches, introduced into the pictures which occupied the most prominent position on the roof of the apse above the high altar, and placed almost on an equality with our Lord, St. Peter, and St. Paul, as in the Church of SS. Cosmas and Damianus at Rome. In the celebrated mosaic of Justinian, at St. Vitalis, Ravenna, the bishop, Maximianus, is habited in his full ecclesiastical robes, including the stole, and carries a cross in his hand. He is accompanied by two priests, one holding a book and the other a censer.

The chief place of honour in the scheme of the decoration of the early basilicas is that occupied by the central figure of the group on the vaulted roof of the apse, and the degradation of symbolism may be traced by noticing the changes which took place from century to century, in the personage selected for this position. In the Churches of SS. Cosmas and Damianus, and of St. Laurence extra Muros at Rome, and St. Vitalis at Ravenna, all of the sixth century, the central figure is Christ. In the Church of St. Agnes at Rome, of the seventh century, it is the patron, St. Agnes. In the Church of St. Maria in Dominica, at Rome, of the ninth century, it is the Virgin and Child, enthroned. Lastly, when the art of mosaic was revived in the twelfth century, the Virgin is placed in this position, seated on a throne, side by side and on an equality with the Saviour, as at St. Maria in Trastevere, at Rome.

Scenes from the Apocalypse, which became so common in Norman sculpture and mediæval MSS., first make their appearance in the mosaics on the west wall of the nave, above the arch of the apse, of the Church of SS. Cosmas and Damianus at Rome, in the sixth century. The representation includes the Agnus Dei, now first associated with the Cross, and the symbols of the four Evangelists. The whole scene is reproduced with but few modifications in the mosaics occupying a similar position in the Church of St. Prassede at Rome, of the ninth century. Palm-trees, and a hand holding a crown above the heads of saints, are characteristic features of the mosaics. We also find the germs of that system of spiritual allegory founded on the characteristics of the animal world, which was subsequently so fully elaborated in the mediæval bestiaries, indicated by the phœnix, typifying Resurrection, in the palm-tree, on the roof of the apse, at SS. Cosmas and Damian. The contrast between the old and new dispensation is symbolised by a procession of twelve sheep, six issuing from the gates of Jerusalem, and six from Bethlehem, one representing the Jews, and the other the Gentiles, placed symmetrically facing each other, on each side of the Agnus Dei, on Mount Zion. We see this first on the frieze round the bottom of the mosaic picture which decorates the roof of the apse of the Church of SS. Cosmas and Damian, of the sixth century, and copies by later artists in the Church of St. Cecilia in Trastevere, of the ninth century, and St. Maria in Trastevere, of the twelfth, all at Rome. The offerings of Abel, Melchisedec, and Abraham, in the Churches of St. Vitalis and St. Apollinare in Classe, at Ravenna, both of the sixth century, are typical of the Sacrament of the Lord's Supper.

The two baptisteries at Ravenna, in the cathedral and in the Church of St. Maria in Cosmedin, both of the sixth century, present us with the earliest representations of the Baptism of Christ in Christian art. The development of the twelfth century type of Christ in Glory, enclosed within a vesica, supported by two or four angels, may be traced back to the disc enclosing the cross, and held by a pair of angels, on the mosaic at St. Vitalis at Ravenna, of the sixth century, which resembles so closely the carvings on the great ivory book-covers at Ravenna, in the Vatican, and in the South Kensington Museum, and also the diptych of Rambona in the Vatican. In the two latter the bust of Christ takes the place of the cross. On the mosaic on the east wall of the nave, above the arch of the apse of the Church of St. Maria in Dominica at Rome, of the ninth century, the whole figure of Christ is enclosed within an oval aureole, supported by an angel on each side.

In the South Kensington Museum there are specimens of small mosaic pictures brought from Italy, and an admirable selection of reproductions of mosaics, full size, which were made by Mr. Caspar Clarke in 1872, by first taking paper casts, and then colouring them by hand. See *Catalogue of Christian Mosaic Pictures in the South Kensington Museum*, by J. W. Appell, 1877; *Report on Mosaic Pictures for Wall Decorations, etc.*, by Mr. Cole and Lieut.-Col. Scott, R.E., 1869.

The chief works containing illustrations of mosaics are as follows:

W. von Salzenberg, *Alt-Christliche Baudenkmale von Constantinopel*, Berlin, 1854 (Mosaics in St. Sophia, Constantinople).

J. H. Parker, *Historical Photographs, illustrative of the Mosaic Pictures in the Churches of Rome.*

R. Garrucci, *Storia del Arte Cristiana*, vol. iv, pls. 204-94.

J. Ciampini, *Vetera Monumenta*, Rome, 1690.

G. B. de Rossi, *Musaici Cristiani*, Rome, 1872.

Gally Knight, *Ecclesiastical Architecture of Italy.*

A complete list of mosaics and subjects will be found in the *Universal Art Inventory*, pt. I, *Mosaics and Stained Glass*, edited by H. Cole, and published by the Science and Art Department, South Kensington Museum.

The following books and articles may be consulted for descriptions, in some cases accompanied by woodcuts.

J. H. Parker, *Mosaic Pictures in Rome and Ravenna.*

H. Barbet de Jouy, *Les Mosaïques Chrétiennes de Rome.*

W. Burges on "Mosaics", in *Gent.'s Mag.*, 1863.

Kugler, *History of Painting*, edited by Eastlake.

L. Vitet, *Etudes sur l'Histoire de l'Art.*

R. St. J. Tyrwhitt, *Art Teaching of the Primitive Church,* chapter on Mosaics.

Martigny's *Dict. des Ant. Chrét.*, article "Mosaïques".

Smith's *Dict. of Christian Ants.*, article "Mosaics".

Crowe and Cavalcaselle, *History of Early Italian Art.*

## LAMPS.

Lamps bearing Christian devices have been found in great numbers in Italy, France, Egypt, and other countries. The use of such articles was either domestic, for giving light in the house; religious, for burning before the shrines of saints or during particular ceremonies; or funereal, for depositing with the body of the deceased. The material of which these lamps are made is either terra-cotta or bronze, the former being the most common. The shape of the terra-cotta lamps is that used by the Romans in pagan times, consisting of a shallow circular bowl covered over at the top, with a spout at one side for the wick, and a handle at the other. The ornament is generally concentrated on the circular top, which is formed into a medallion, surrounded sometimes by a border of smaller ones. The subjects correspond with those found on the paintings in the Catacombs and on the sculptured sarcophagi, such as the Good Shepherd, Jonah and the Whale, Jonah and the Gourd, the sacred monogram, etc.[1] The style of the art is classical. The decorative treatment of the metal lamps is different, and consists in making the body of the vessel in the form of some object of devotion, such as the ship of the church or a basilica; or in making the handle like a circular disc with the sacred monogram or Jonah upon it, or like a cross, or the head of a bird, or a lamb. Garrucci, in his *Storia del Arte Cristiana*, vol. vi, pls. 473-76, illustrates a large number of these objects, and their use is described in Martigny's *Dict. des Ant. Chrét.*, art. "Lampes Chrétiennes".

## Holy Oil Vessels.

*Seventh Century.*—In early Christian times it was generally believed that oil which had been burnt in lamps before the shrines of saints, or in the holy places at Jerusalem, acquired a peculiar sanctity, and it was therefore carefully collected on cotton-wool and enclosed in little vials, so as to be available, when required, for unction on certain days, or for effecting miraculous cures.[2] The Popes used to send these holy oils as a special mark of favour to sovereigns and other distinguished personages; the most remarkable instance being those collected by Abbot John, in the days of St. Gregory the Great (A.D. 600), and sent to Theodolinda, Queen of the Lombards, which are still preserved in the treasury of the Cathedral of Monza, together with the catalogue, written on papyrus, commencing thus:

"Nōt de olea scōrum martirum qui Romæ in corpore requiescunt id est."

Then follow the names of the shrines of the sixty-five saints from which the oils were obtained, arranged in two columns, and it concludes:—" Quas olea sca temporibs domini Gregorii papæ adduxit Johannes indignus et preccátor dominæ Theodolindæ,

---

[1] With the addition of the Two Spies carrying the Bunch of Grapes, and Christ treading on the Asp and the Basilisk.

[2] Oil merely placed in vessels near sacred localities, or in any other way associated with them, was considered equally efficacious.

reginæ de Roma."[1] Most of the vessels in which the holy oils are enclosed are of glass, but some are of metal, and ornamented with figures in relief. They are shaped like a circular flask with flat sides, and have a short neck at the top, ornamented with a cross. Almost all have Greek inscriptions, either running round the edge or written horizontally across the side, having reference to the use of the vessels, such as:

ΕΛΕΟΝ (for ΕΛΑΙΟΝ) ΞΤΛΟΤ ΖΩΗC ΤΩΝ ΑΓΙΩΝ ΧΡΙCΤΟΤ ΤΟΠΩΝ

("Oil of the wood of life of the holy places of Christ").
Or—
ΕΤΛΟΓΙΑ ΚΤΡΙΟΤ ΤΩΝ ΑΓΙΩΝ ΤΟΠΩΝ
("The blessing of the holy places of the Lord").

In some cases there are inscriptions descriptive of the scenes represented. The subjects are as follows:

(1) Annunciation.
(1) Salutation.
(1) Nativity.
(3) Adoration of the Magi (ΜΑΓΟΙ, "The Magi").
(1) Baptism of Christ.
(7) Crucifixion with the Two Thieves.
(7) Two Maries and Angel at the Sepulchre (ΑΝΕCΤΙΟ ΧΤΡΟC, "The Resurrection of the Lord").
(4) Ascension (ΕΜΜΑΝΟΤΗΛ ΜΕΘ ΗΜΩΝ Ο ΘΕΟC, "Emmanuel God with us").
Cross.
Heads of Twelve Apostles.
Christ and Twelve Apostles (Ο K̄C̄ ΜΟΤ ΚΑΙ Ο ΘΕΟC ΜΟΤ, "My Lord and my God").

The style of the art is Byzantine, and the treatment of the subjects is worthy of very careful examination, as some of them mark the transition between the forms found on the sculptured sarcophagi and those which continued in use down to the end of the twelfth century.

The Crucifixion and the Maries at the Sepulchre on these vessels should be compared with the representations on the

[1] Frisi, *Memorie della Chiese Monzese*, vol. ii, p. 63; and Marini, *Papiri Diplomatici*, p. 327.

Norman font at Lenton, near Nottingham, as they possess many features in common. The scenes which occur with greatest frequency on the holy oil vessels are,—the Crucifixion, the Maries at the Sepulchre, the Ascension, and Adoration of the Magi. In the latter, the Virgin is shown with the nimbus round the head, seated on a throne, holding the Infant Saviour on her lap; on the right are three shepherds; and on the left, the three Magi, with Phrygian caps; above the head of the Virgin is the star, to which two angels are pointing; below are the shepherds' flocks. The treatment of the Crucifixion is most peculiar, Christ not being represented, as is usually the case, upon the cross; but His bust, with the cruciferous nimbus round the head, and Sol and Luna on each side, is placed above a small cross, at the foot of which are two kneeling figures. In one instance the cross is omitted, and our Lord has His arms, from the elbow to the hand, stretched out at right angles to the body. In all cases the two thieves are represented bound by the feet to a cross, the horizontal bar of which is considerably below the level of the shoulders. In the Ascension the figure of Christ is enclosed within an aureole, and the treatment is almost exactly the same as that found in the Saxon MSS. and in twelfth century art.

Besides the holy oil vessels brought from Jerusalem, others came from Egypt, on which are portrayed the martyr Mennas of the Diocletian persecution, whose shrine, not far from Alexandria, was the object of numerous pilgrimages. One found at Arles[1] has upon it the figure of St. Mennas, with hands outstretched in the ancient attitude of prayer, and a beast on each side crouching at his feet. It is inscribed:

## ΕΥΛΟΓΙΑ ΤΟΥ ΑΓΙΟΥ ΜΗΝΑ

("The blessing of St. Mennas"). Many similar ones are preserved in the museums at London, Paris, Florence, and Turin. Illustrations of twelve holy oil vessels will be found in Garrucci's *Storia del Arte Cristiana*, vol. vi, pls. 433 to 435; and their use is fully described in Martigny's *Dict. des. Ant. Chrét.* (art. "Huiles Saintes"), and Smith's *Dict. of Christian Ants.* (art. "Oils—holy").

---

[1] Martigny's *Dict.*, p. 346.

## Holy Water Vessels.

This is not the place to discuss the various uses to which holy water was put by the Church from the earliest times; but the vessels in which it was contained, being ornamented with symbolical devices, cannot pass unnoticed. Some of the most ancient examples are vases of lead or marble, and the later ones, little *situlæ* or buckets of ivory, or wood with metal fittings. Those belonging to the former class usually bore Greek inscriptions having reference to their use, such as the curious sentence which reads equally well backwards or forwards—

ΝΙΨΟΝ ΑΝΟΜΗΜΑΤΑ ΜΗ ΜΟΝΑΝ ΟΨΙΝ

("Wash thine iniquities, not thy face only").

This seems to have been a well-recognised formula in the Eastern Church, being found on vases discovered at Constantinople and Autun, in France, and it has been carved on fonts in England at Sandbach in Cheshire (date 1667); Rufford in Lancashire, and St. Bartholomew's, Sydenham, near London. A marble vase, brought from Greece, and preserved in the Church of SS. Mark and Andrew in the island of Murano, near Venice,[1] has upon it the text from Isaiah (xii, 3)—

ΑΝΤΛΗΣΑΤΑΙ ΤΔΩΡ ΜΕΤΑ ΣΤΦΡΟΣΤΝΗΣ ΟΤΙ ΦΩΝΗ K̄T̄ ΕΠΙ ΤΩΝ ΤΔΑΤΩΝ.

But far the most interesting specimen is one from Tunis,[2] also bearing the first four words of the foregoing inscription, and ornamented, in addition, with the following Christian subjects: Two stags drinking from the Four Rivers of Paradise, issuing from Mount Zion; the Good Shepherd; Angel holding palm and crown to Orante; pair of peacocks drinking from vase; palm-trees; border of vines. The style of the art is classical, and the subjects correspond with those found on the sculptured sarcophagi.

Two very curious holy water buckets, ornamented with Scrip-

---

[1] Martigny's *Dict.*, p. 263.
[2] *Ibid.*, p. 264; and Garrucci, *Storia del Arte Cristiana*, vol. vi, pl. 428.

ture scenes, have been found in connection with burials; one in a Merovingian cemetery at Miannay, near Abbeville, in France,[1] and another in a Saxon grave at Long Whittenham, in Berkshire.[2] The subjects of the Miannay bucket, which has embossed gilt copper mountings, are as follows: Christ treading on the Serpent; Temptation of Adam and Eve; Daniel in the Lions' Den and Habakkuk; Habakkuk lifted up by the hair of the head, inscribed—

> (ANGE)LVS MISS(VS)
> DANIEL PROFETA
> ABACV FERT (PANEM)
> IN LACV LEONVM

The Long Whittenham bucket is like those found in the pagan Saxon graves, formed of staves and hoops, with ornamental designs on *repoussée* plates of metal. It is 6 inches high, and 4½ inches in diameter. The body with which it was associated was that of a boy, buried with the head lying to the west. At his feet was a bronze kettle, on the breast a small iron knife; close to the right foot a spear-head point, downwards; and on the right of the head the bucket in question. The subjects represented upon it are as follows: The Chi-Rho monogram, and the Alpha and Omega within a circle; the Miracle of Cana; the Baptism of Christ, inscribed IΩANNHC; the Annunciation. This precious object is now preserved in the Mayer collection in the Liverpool Museum.

The ivory *situlæ* are fully described in Professor Westwood's *Catalogue of the Fictile Ivories in the South Kensington Museum*, p. 266. The best typical specimens are those in the Duomo at Milan, and in Mr. Attenborough's collection, both inscribed and ornamented with Scriptural subjects, the former having been made for Otho II by Gotfred, Archbishop of Milan (A.D. 973-78), and the latter for Otho III (born A.D. 980). Casts of these are to be seen in the South Kensington Museum.

---

[1] Ed. Le Blant, *Inscr. Chrét. de la Gaule*, vol. i, pl. 251; and in *Mém. de la Soc. des Ant. de France*, vol. xxxv, p. 68; also *Proc. Soc. Ant. Scot.*, vol. xi, pl. 16.

[2] *Archæologia*, vol. xxxviii, p. 327.

## Belt-clasps from Burgundian and Frankish Graves.

In a previous course of Rhind Lectures,[1] Dr. Joseph Anderson has referred to the remarkable representations of Daniel in the Lions' Den, which occur upon certain belt-clasps found in the ancient Burgundian and Frankish cemeteries of Switzerland and Savoy. The graves from which these objects are obtained are formed of large slabs of undressed stone, placed in a north-west and south-east direction, and contained damascened weapons, personal ornaments, and fragments of coarse pottery. The age of the burials is not known with any degree of certainty, but from the fact of their being Christian,[2] and from the character of the lettering of the inscriptions, it is not probable that any of them are earlier than the sixth century. The belt-clasps are made of bronze, in some cases encrusted with silver, and the average size is four inches long by two inches and a half wide. The buckle is of the ordinary shape used at the present day, and the flat part, which is attached to the leather, is ornamented with engraving very rudely executed. The subjects, which are in some cases explained by inscriptions, are as follows :—

*Daniel in the Lions' Den, with hands upraised in the ancient attitude of prayer, between two lions who are licking his feet.* Example from Lavigny, in Lausanne Museum, inscribed NAS-ALDVS NANSA VIVAT DEO VTERE FELIX DANINIL; also from Dailleus, inscribed DAGNINILD DVO LEONES PEDES EIVS LENGEBANT; and four others without inscriptions from Mongifi, Sévery, Blye, and Villecin.

*Daniel in the Lions' Den, shown in a similar manner, but with Habakkuk or another figure.* Example from Mâcon, now in the Museum at St. Germain, inscribed DANIEL PROFETA ABACV PROFETA; and another from St. Maur, inscribed RENATVS DEACONVS VIVAT CVM PACE ANNVS CENTVM.

*Figure in ancient attitude of prayer between two beasts rampant.* Examples from Arnex and Montillier, in Lausanne Museum.

---

[1] *Scotland in Early Christian Times* (2nd Series), p. 147; also see *Proc. Soc. Ant. Scot.*, vol. ii, p. 363.

[2] Clovis, the first of the Frankish kings of the Merovingian Dynasty, was baptised A.D. 486, and the Burgundians became Christians in the sixth century.

*Figures in ancient attitude of prayer, without accessories.* Examples from Bofflens and Tolchenaz, in the Lausanne Museum, and from Villechevreux and Balme.

*Cross in the centre, with man and sea-monster on each side.* Examples from Echallens, Marnens, and Bofflens, in Lausanne Museum.

Descriptions and illustrations of all these belt-clasps will be found in the following works:

Ed. Le Blant, *Inscriptions Chrétiennes de la Gaule*, vol. i, p. 493, and vol. ii, pls. 42 and 43.

Ed. Le Blant, "Note sur quelques représentations antiques de Daniel dans la Fosse aux Lions." *Mém. de la Soc. des Ant. de France*, vol. xxxv, p. 68.

F. Troyon, "Bracelets et Agrafes antiques." *Mittheilungen der Antiquarischen Gessellschaft in Zürich*, vol. ii, pl. 3.

E. Clerc, *Essai sur l'histoire de la Franche Comté à l'époque Romaine.*

De Surigny, *Agrafes Chrétiennes Mérovingiennes.*

## IVORIES.

Under the heading of ivories are included all carvings executed in bone, walrus-tusk, or other substances of a like nature. From the third or fourth century, down to the time of the Reformation, the Church employed this extremely beautiful and durable material, wherever it was possible, in the decoration of objects connected with Christian worship, such as the following: (1) Ecclesiastical Diptychs; (2) Devotional Triptychs; (3) Book-covers; (4) Caskets or Reliquaries; (5) Pyxes; (6) Situlæ; (7) Liturgical Combs; (8) Flabella; (9) Pastoral Staves; (10) Paxes; (11) Episcopal Chairs; (12) Crucifixes; (13) Images.

In addition to the above, it will be found that secular objects occasionally bear Christian devices, as for instance: (1) Tenure Horns; (2) Chessmen; (3) Draughtsmen; (4) Seals; (5) Mirror Cases.

The style of art exhibited in ivory carvings varies according to the period and locality. The earliest examples resemble the classical sculptures on the sarcophagi at Rome,—as, for instance, the celebrated Brescia Casket, of the fifth or sixth century,[1] on which we find the stories of Jonah and Daniel, treated just in the same manner as in the Catacomb paintings. In the sixth century Classical art was superseded by Byzantine, and on the great book-cover in the Vatican Library[2] two angels are to be seen supporting a circular disc enclosing the cross, exactly corresponding with the mosaics in the Church of St. Vitalis at Ravenna[3] (A.D. 547). On the South Kensington book-cover[4] the bust of Christ occupies the same position as the Cross on that in the Vatican, and from this was developed the vesica supported by angels, and enclosing the full-length figure of the Saviour, which is so common in the twelfth century, both in the illuminated MSS. and on the sculptured tympana of Norman doorways. The most important work in ivory belonging to the sixth century is the chair made by Maximian,[5] Archbishop of Ravenna (A.D. 546-556), and now in the cathedral at that place, ornamented with plaques illustrating the lives of Joseph and of Our Lord. After this time a marked decline took place in ivory sculpture, but in the middle of the eighth century the art again revived under the auspices of Charlemagne (A.D. 768-814), who took advantage of the iconoclastic quarrels raging in the East (A.D. 750-867) to employ such workmen as were compelled to emigrate to the West, in consequence of the persecutions at Constantinople.

The ivory carvings now existing of the Carlovingian School belong chiefly to the ninth and tenth centuries, the most authentically dated specimens being the plaques forming the covers of the Psalter and the Evangeliarium of Charles the Bald[6] in the National Library at Paris. The Carlovingian style is distinguished by the peculiar acanthus foliage which is introduced in the borders,[7] by simplicity of composition, and absence of any highly ornamental features.

Ivories of the eleventh and twelfth centuries are chiefly

[1] Westwood's *Catalogue of Fictile Ivories in S. K. Mus.*, p. 36.
[2] *Ibid.*, p. 51 ; and Garrucci, *Storia del Arte Cristiana*, vol. vi, pl. 457.
[3] Parker's *Mosaic Pictures in Rome*, p. 111.
[4] Westwood, *Catal.*, p. 52.
[5] *Ibid.*, p. 31 ; and *Garrucci*, vol. vi, pls. 414 to 423.
[6] Westwood's *Catal.*, p. 102.
[7] See Westwood's *Catal.*, pls. 11, 19, 23.

German or French, showing Byzantine and Carlovingian influence, after which period the Gothic style was introduced universally, except in the Greek Church.

Ivories which can be shown to be Saxon, Irish, or Scandinavian, either by the ornament, inscriptions, or other features, are of the greatest rarity, the following being those which are at present known.[1]

### Anglo-Saxon.

South Kensington Museum. No. 142-66, Plaque, with Adoration of the Magi.

S. K. Mus. No. 3-72, Plaque, with Descent from the Cross.

Cambridge Antiquarian Museum. Cast in S. K. Mus. No. 90-73, Westwood, *Catal.*, p. 138; Plaque, with Christ showing His wounds; found at Elmham, Norfolk. Inscribed in Saxon capitals.

British Museum. Seal of Godwin, a thane, and Godgytha, a nun. Inscribed in Saxon capitals.

### Hiberno-Saxon.

Brussels Museum. Diptych from Church of St. Martin, at Genoels Elderen, Limburg. Westwood, *Catal.*, p. 479; Christ treading on the Asp and the Basilisk; Annunciation and Salutation. Inscribed in Saxon capitals.

Head of Pastoral Staff, found at Aghadoe Cathedral, in Ireland, with man being devoured by the Serpent forming the volute.

### Scandinavian.

British Museum. Franks Casket. Cast in S. K. Mus. 240-73, Westwood, *Catal.*, p. 234; with Adoration of Magi, and Flight of Jews from Jerusalem. Inscribed with Runes.

Copenhagen Museum. Cross of Princess Gunhilda, niece of King Canute (died A.D. 1076). Cast in S. K. Mus. No. 102-73, Westwood, *Catal.*, p. 152; with Christ showing His wounds.

The following Caskets have Scandinavian ornament, but no figure-subjects.

Munich Museum. Casket of Cunigunda. Cast in S. K. Mus. No. 42-73, Westwood, *Catal.*, p. 336.

---

[1] A bone casket with interlaced work, belonging to Miss Drysdale of Kircaldy, is illustrated in the *Proc. Soc. Ant. Scot.*, vol. xx, p. 390.

Cathedral of Cammin, in Pomerania. Reliquary of St. Cordula. Cast in S. K. Mus. No. 59-72, Westwood, *Catal.*, p. 336.

Brunswick Museum. Nethii's Casket. Cast in S. K. Mus. No. 366-73, Westwood, *Catal.*, p. 335. Inscribed in Runes.

*Diptychs.*—A diptych means anything folded together double (from the Greek δίπτυχον), the word being generally applied to the two-leaved tablets of wood or ivory on which the ancients used to write their memoranda. The inner faces of the diptychs were hollowed out into the form of a shallow tray, which was filled with wax, presenting a surface on which the owner could write his notes with a style, sharp-pointed at one end, but blunt at the other end for making erasures. The two leaves were fastened together by a hinge, consisting of two or three loops of wire threaded through holes in each side. When the leaves were shut the writing was protected from injury, and the outside was usually ornamented with carving.

The tablets used by private individuals were of small size, and made of common wood, but in the later days of the Roman Empire it was the custom for Consuls on their appointment to make presents to important personages of elaborately carved ivory diptychs of much larger dimensions, varying from 4 to 6 inches in width, and from 12 to 15 inches in length.

Most of the Consular diptychs bear inscriptions which enable the date to be fixed, and some are ornamented with Christian symbols, so that the light thus thrown on the history of early art is of very great value. Prof. Westwood has compiled a list of twenty-one Consular diptychs, still in existence, ranging in date from A.D. 248 to 541, which will be found given in W. Maskell's *Handbook of Ivories in the South Kensington Museum* (p. 28). Some of the best of these are in the British Museum, the South Kensington Museum, and the Mayer Museum at Liverpool, and the rest abroad.

The Consular diptychs with Christian symbols are as follows:

A.D. 406.—Of Anicius Probus, in Aosta Cathedral. The Emperor Honorius, with nimbus round head, holding a labarum, inscribed: "IN NOMINI X̄P̄I VINCAS SEMPER."

A.D. 505.—Of Fl. Theodorus Valentinianus, in the Berlin Museum. The bust of Christ, with cruciferous nimbus within a circular medallion. (Westwood, *Catal. of Ivories in S. K. Mus.*, p. 17.)

A.D. 506.—Of Flavius Dalagaiphus Areobindus, in the Lucca Library. The Cross. (Gori, *Thesaurus Diptychorum*, vol. i, pl. 8.)

A.D. 513.—Of Flavius Taurus Clementinus, in the Mayer Museum at Liverpool. The Cross between medallions enclosing busts of the reigning emperor and empress.

A.D. 516.—Of Flavius Petrus Justinianus, in the Paris Library. The Cross at the beginning and end of the inscription. (Millin, *Voyages*, vol. i, pl. 19.)

A.D. 517.—Of Fl. Anastasius Paulus Probus Pompeius, in the Paris Library. The Cross at the beginning and end of the inscription. (Labarte, *Hist. Arts Industr.*—Album, pl. 3.)

Of the same Consul, in the South Kensington Museum.

A.D. 530.—Of Rufinus Gennadius Orestes, in the South Kensington Museum. The Cross between busts of the Emperor Justinian and the Empress Theodora. (*Gori*, vol. ii, pl. 17.)

A.D. 541.—Of Anicius Faustus Albinus Basilius, in the Uffizii at Florence. Ball and Cross held by the Consul. (*Gori*, vol. ii, pl. 20.)

It is supposed that in the time of the Roman Empire the Consular diptychs contained the *Fasti Consulares*, or list of all the preceding officials who had acted as Consuls; but many of these tablets were applied subsequently to ecclesiastical purposes, and were then inscribed with the names of the newly baptised, benefactors of the Church, saints, martyrs, etc., which were read out at Mass. One of the best examples of a Consular diptych, applied to the use of the Church, is that of Flavius Taurus Clementinus, in the Mayer Museum at Liverpool.[1] The diptych of Fl. Anastasius Paulus Probus Pompeius in the Paris Library, contains a list of the Bishops of Bourges; and another Roman diptych, of the sixth century, in the Cathedral of Novara, has a similar list of bishops of that place, from St. Gaudentius to A.D. 1170. The Consular diptych of Flavius Anicius Justinianus Augustus, in the Paris Library, contains litanies of the ninth century and the names of saints. Perhaps the most remarkable

---

[1] Engraved in *Gori*, vol. i, pl. 10; inscription and translation given in Maskell's *S. K. Handbook of Ivories*, p. 38.

instance of a Consular diptych put to ecclesiastical use is that at Monza, which was presented to the Empress Theodolinda by St. Gregory the Great, having upon it representations of St. Gregory and King David.[1]

Besides the Consular diptychs there are also purely ecclesiastical ones, which had never been used previously for secular purposes, ornamented with Christian devices, as, for instance, the very interesting one of Rambona, in the Vatican,[2] and many others. Sometimes diptychs have been utilised as book-covers at a later period.

*Triptychs.*—The name triptych is applied to any set of three ivory panels hinged twice, so as to fold together. Objects of this class are employed in the same way as devotional pictures, being placed upright, with the two side-wings open, and inclined at equal angles to the central plaque, so that the religious subjects carved on the three inner faces can be seen. Most triptychs are of the thirteenth and fourteenth centuries, but they are mentioned by Anastasius in the *Liber Pontificalis* as early as A.D. 772, and there is in the Paris Library one of the finest Greek Byzantine triptychs known of the eleventh century.[3]

*Book-Covers.*—The volumes of the Gospels, the Psalters, and other books used by the Church, were very frequently ornamented with ivory plaques carved with Scripture subjects. Many of the MSS. still in existence retain their original bindings, there being an especially fine collection in the Paris Library. The oldest ivory book-covers which have been preserved belong to the sixth or seventh centuries, and are generally of large size, about 15 ins. by 12 ins., composed of five oblong plaques, one in the centre and the four others forming a kind of frame round it. There is a splendid specimen of a book-cover of this class in the South Kensington Museum, and casts of four other similar ones from Milan, Ravenna, the Vatican, and

---

[1] Engraved in Martigny's *Dict. des Ant. Chrét.*, art. "Diptyques", p. 255.
[2] Westwood, *Catal. of Fictile Ivories in S. K. Mus.*, p. 56.
[3] Cast in S. K. Mus. Westwood, *Catal.*, p. 83. Another example of the same date, from the Soltykoff Collection, is figured in Labarte's *Album*, pl. 11.

Paris, all of which are engraved in Garrucci, *Storia del Arte Cristiana*, and described in Professor Westwood's *Catalogue*. These are all extremely interesting specimens of early Christian art, and the top panel is, in most of them, occupied by a pair of angels, supporting a circular disc enclosing the bust of the Saviour, as on the Rambona diptych in the Vatican; or the Cross, as on the mosaics at St. Vitalis at Ravenna. Many of the later book-covers are in single plaques of small size, with the Crucifixion or Christ in Glory. The ivory cover of the Psalter of the Princess Melisenda of Jerusalem, in the British Museum,[1] of the twelfth century, is most beautifully ornamented with delicate carving, representing scenes from the life of King David on one side, and the Six Acts of Mercy on the other.

*Caskets.*—Reliquaries and boxes used for ecclesiastical purposes are often ornamented with ivory plaques, having Scripture subjects carved upon them, one of the oldest being the celebrated Brescia casket,[2] which is in the style of the sculptured sarcophagi. The shape of these caskets is either rectangular, or sometimes the top is made with sloping sides like the roof of a house, as in the case of the Carlovingian casket of the tenth century in the Louvre.[3] The Franks casket in the British Museum, Nethii's casket in the Brunswick Museum, the casket of Cunigunda in the Munich Museum, and the reliquary of St. Cordula in the Cathedral of Cammin, in Pomerania, are all Scandinavian, and of the greatest interest.

*Pyxes.*—Small cylindrical boxes which were used by priests for carrying about the consecrated wafer, to be used at the Sacrament, are called pyxes. The earliest of these objects date back to about the fifth century, as, for instance, the one at Milan Cathedral, with the story of Jonah treated as on the sculptured sarcophagi. An ivory pyx of the sixth century, in the British Museum, is remarkable as having carved upon it scenes from the legendary life of St. Mennas, being probably the first instance of a representation of the kind.

---

[1] Westwood, *Catal.*, p. 73.  [2] *Ibid.*, p. 36.
[3] *Ibid.*, p. 230.

*Situlæ.*— Buckets for holding holy water are called *situlæ* and have been already described.

*Combs.*—The liturgical comb was used formerly for dressing the hair of the bishop before celebrating High Mass, and formed one of the regular ceremonial properties of the Church. The earliest examples have teeth on one side only, and are sometimes ornamented with Christian figure-subjects; two of the finest being that of St. Herebert, in the Cologne Museum,[1] of the ninth century, with the Crucifixion upon it; and the comb of St. Lupus, in the Cathedral at Sens.[2]

*Flabella.*—The ceremonial fan, or flabellum, with which the flies were brushed away from the elements used at the Sacrament of the Mass in hot weather, often had an ivory case and handle carved with Scripture subjects, but such objects are by no means common.[3]

*Pastoral Staves.*—The volutes of pastoral staves are often made of ivory, in the form of a serpent, with the Agnus Dei in the centre.[4] A curious Irish example, found at Aghadoe Cathedral, has been already referred to.

*Paxes.*—When the custom of giving the kiss of peace between the members of the Christian community fell into disuse, the ceremony of kissing a small figure sculptured on marble or ivory was substituted. Martigny, in his *Dict. des Ant. Chrét.* (art. "Paix"), gives an engraving of a pax of the eighth century in the Church of Cividale, in Frioul, which he states is the oldest now in existence. It has an ivory plaque in the centre with the Crucifixion. There is in the Berlin Museum a pax of the twelfth century, with the decapitation and burial of St. John upon it.[5] These objects are of great rarity.

---

[1] Westwood, *Catal.*, p. 315.

[2] Cahier and Martin, *Nouveaux Mélanges d'Archéologie*, p. 72.

[3] See Westwood's *Catal.*, p. 61; and Didron's *Annales Archéologiques*, vol. xiii, p. 40.

[4] See Cahier and Martin, *Mélanges d'Archéologie*, vol. iv, p. 198.

[5] Westwood, *Catal.*, p. 276.

*Episcopal Chairs.*—The two most celebrated ivory chairs are the chair of Maximianus, Archbishop of Ravenna A.D. 549, preserved in the cathedral at Ravenna,[1] having upon it scenes from the Lives of Christ and of Joseph; and the chair of St. Peter at Rome,[2] ornamented with the Labours of Hercules.

*Images and Crucifixes.*—Both images and crucifixes of early date are exceedingly uncommon.

The chief collections of ivories in this country are to be found in the British Museum, the South Kensington Museum, the Bodleian Library and Ashmolean Museum at Oxford, and the Mayer Museum in Liverpool.

A magnificent series of casts of ivories from most of the foreign collections is displayed in the South Kensington Museum, and has been admirably catalogued and described by Professor Westwood. The Arundel Society also sell a set of casts of early Christian ivories.

Illustrations of a large number of ivories will be found in the following works:

R. Garrucci, *Storia del Arte Cristiana*, vol. vi, pls. 414-456.

Labarte, *Histoire des Arts Industriels du Moyen Age*—Album.

J. B. Waring, *Art Treasures exhibited at Manchester*.

Cahier and Martin, *Nouveaux Mélanges d'Archéologie*.

Didron, *Annales Archéologiques*.

Gori, *Thesaurus Diptychorum*.

Westwood, *Catalogue of Fictile Ivories in the South Kensington Museum*.

Maskell, *Catalogue of Ivories in the South Kensington Museum*.

There is at present no really good text-book dealing with the subject of ivories as a whole, but the following short accounts may be read with advantage:

Sir M. Digby Wyatt, *Notices of Sculpture in Ivory*.

Professor Westwood, *Ivory Carvings*.

W. Maskell, *Ivories: South Kensington Art Handbook*.

---

[1] Garrucci, *Storia del Arte Cristiana*, vol. vi, plates 414-422.

[2] *Archæologia*, vol. xlv, p. 426; and *Vetusta Monumenta*, vol. vi.

## Church Doors.

Many of the doors of the Cathedrals abroad are of great size, and made to fold back in two leaves, which are divided up into rectangular panels, ornamented with scenes from Scripture. Most of these doors belong to the eleventh and twelfth centuries,[1] and attention is called to them here, not because they preceded the introduction of Christianity into Great Britain, but as presenting several complete series of Old and New Testament subjects similar to those found in the contemporary MSS., which are of the utmost value for the sake of comparison with Norman sculptures of the same period. It may here be pointed out that in the early stages of Christian art in the Catacombs and on the sculptured sarcophagi, the subjects are mixed together quite irrespective of their historical order of sequence, and it was not until the art of miniature-painting in the MSS. had attained considerable development that we get a regular series illustrating any particular part of the Bible, such as the first part of Genesis or the Life of Christ. In arranging the scheme of the decoration of a church, it will be found that only certain portions of the building and its fittings are adapted, by the shape of the surface presented, to receive a long series of pictures following each other in succession.

The north and south walls of the nave were chosen in the early basilicas for the Old and New Testament histories, but in the twelfth century, when the interior wall-space was more broken up with openings, the large doors offered better scope for decoration of this kind; and although the scale of the figures was smaller in the latter case, they were in a more favourable position for being seen, both as being nearer the ground and in front of the spectator, instead of to his right or left.

Good examples of metal church-doors, with panels of Scripture subjects, exist at the following places :—

Executed in the eleventh century : Amalfi Cathedral, Italy (A.D. 1066); Augsburg Cathedral, Bavaria (A.D. 1070) ; Hildes-

---

[1] The doors of the Church of S. Sabina at Rome are executed in the style of the early ivories of the sixth century. (See Garrucci, *Storia del Arte Cristiana*, vol. vi, pl. 499.)

heim Cathedral, Prussia (A.D. 1015); Monte Cassino, Italy (A.D. 1066); Monte Gargano, Italy (A.D. 1076); Church of St. Paul extra Muros, Rome (A.D. 1070), now destroyed.

Executed in the twelfth century: St. Nicholas Church, Bari, Italy; Benvenuto Cathedral, Italy (A.D. 1150); Monreale Cathedral, Sicily (A.D. 1179); Novgorod Cathedral, Russia (A.D. 1171); Pisa Cathedral, Italy (A.D. 1180); Ravello Cathedral, Italy (A.D. 1179); Church of San Zenone, Verona, Italy.

All of the foregoing are of cast-bronze, with the figures in relief, except the doors at the Church of St. Paul extra Muros at Rome, where the workmanship is of the kind known as *agemina*, or metal inlaid with silver wire.

In a few rare instances, doors with panels of carved wood, illustrating the Bible, have survived, as in the Church of St. Maria am Capitol, at Cologne, Prussia; and in the Churches of Abu Sargah and Sitt Miriam, at Cairo, Egypt.

In Northern Europe and in England there are a few examples of Christian figure-subjects on the ironwork of church-doors, as at Versäs, in Vestergöthland, Sweden[1]; Stillingfleet, Yorkshire[2]; Sempringham, Lincolnshire[3]; Staplehurst, Kent.[4]

There are casts in the South Kensington Museum of the doors at Augsburg, Hildesheim, and Cologne.

Illustrations of some of these doors will be found in the following works:

J. Gailhabaud, *L'Architecture du $V^{me}$ au $XVII^{me}$ Siècle*. Doors at Verona and Cologne.

Seroux d'Agincourt, *L'Art par les Monuments*. Door in the Church of St. Paul extra Muros, Rome.

F. Adelung, *Die Korschionschen Thüren, etc., Novgorod.*

J. Von Allioli, *Die Bronze-Thüre des Domes zu Augsburg.*

The Egyptian wood-carvings are of very special interest. Those from Sitt Miriam, at Cairo, are now in the British Museum, and other similar ones are described and illustrated in Butler's *Coptic Churches of Egypt*. The subjects on the panels from Sitt Miriam are: Entry into Jerusalem; Baptism of Christ

---

[1] Oscar Montelius, *Sveriges Historia*, vol. i, p. 481.
[2] Raymond Bordeaux, *Serrurie du Moyen Age*, pl. xl.
[3] Brandon's *Analysis of Gothic Architecture*.
[4] *Archæologia Cantiana*, vol. ix, p. 191.

and Annunciation; Descent of the Holy Spirit; Nativity (with the washing after birth); Ascension; Harrowing of Hell; Five Crosses. Those on the panels at Abu Sargah: Nativity; Three Saints on horseback; Last Supper.

The saints on horseback, one of which bears a striking resemblance to the figure on the sculpture over the doorway at Fordington Church in Dorsetshire, will be referred to in a future lecture. The nimbus of Christ in the scene of the Entry into Jerusalem on the Sitt Miriam panels is marked with a cross, which peculiarity occurs in the *Book of Kells*, and on some of the Isle of Man crosses.

## MSS.

The earliest MSS. executed in this country are either Irish or Saxon, and do not date back beyond the seventh century. The foreign MSS., previous to the introduction of the art of illumination into England, may be divided into three classes, according to the style of the art of the miniatures: (1) those in the classical style; (2) those in the Byzantine; and (3) those in the Carlovingian. Illustrated MSS. of the Bible in the classical style are of the greatest possible rarity, the only known examples being—

The Greek Genesis in the Imperial Library at Vienna, containing forty-eight miniatures explanatory of the text (see Garrucci, *Storia del Arte Cristiana*, vol. iii, pls. 112-123; and Seroux d'Agincourt, *L'Art par les Monuments*, vol. iv, pt. 1, pl. 19).

The Greek Genesis of the sixth century, in the British Museum (Otho B. vi), originally containing 250 small square miniatures, most of which were destroyed in the Cottonian fire in 1731, those remaining being engraved in *Vetusta Monumenta*, vol. i, pl. 67.

*The History of Joshua*, in the Vatican Library, of the seventh or eighth century (see *Garrucci*, vol. iii, pls. 157-167; *D'Agincourt*, vol. iv, pt. 1, pl. 28).

The earliest illuminations in the Byzantine style are in the Syriac Gospels in the Laurentian Library at Florence, written by Rabula in A.D. 586, containing a large number of marginal drawings of scenes from the Old and New Testament, and the first known representation of the Crucifixion (see A. M. Biscioni, *Bibliothecæ Medico Laurentianæ Catalogus*; *D'Agincourt*, vol. iv, pt. 1, pl. 27; *Garrucci*, vol. iii, pl. 156).

·The Greek Gospels seldom have any pictures except the portraits of the four Evangelists. The most valuable series of Byzantine drawings of Scripture subjects in England[1] is to be found in the Greek Psalter in the British Museum (Add. MS. No. 19,352), written A.D. 1066, which is a perfect mine of information on early Christian art (see Waagen, *Treasures of Art in England*, Suppl., p. 7).

The principal Carlovingian MSS., containing illustrations of the Old Testament, are as follows :—The Alchuine Bible, of the ninth century, in the British Museum (Add. MS. No. 10,546), with pictures of Adam and Eve, Moses, Four Evangelists, and Agnus Dei. The Bible of St. Paul's extra Muros at Rome, of the ninth century, with scenes from lives of Adam and Eve, Moses, David (see *D'Agincourt*, vol. iv, pl. 42; and the *Bible of the Monastery of St. Paul's at Rome*, text by I. O. Westwood, and thirty-eight photos, published by J. H. Parker). The Bible presented to Charles the Bald by Count Vivian, of the ninth century, in the Paris Library, with scenes from lives of Adam and Eve, Moses, and David, at the beginning of Genesis, Exodus, and the Psalms (see Dibdin's *Tour in France and Germany*, vol. ii, 156). The Psalter of Charles the Bald, of the ninth century, in the Paris Library.

The illuminated Carlovingian MSS. of the Gospels are:— The Codex Aureus in the British Museum (Harl. 2788), of the ninth century; the Gospels of St. Medard of Soissons, of the eighth century, in the Paris Library, with a picture of the mystic fountain, the Evangelistiarium of Charlemagne (A.D. 781), in the Paris Library, with the mystic fountain; Otfrid's Paraphrase of the Gospels, in the Vienna Library, of the ninth century, with the entry into Jerusalem (see Westwood's *Palæographia Pictoria Sacra*).

There is no Celtic MS. at present known which contains drawings illustrating the Old Testament; and the only Saxon

---

[1] The Paris Library possesses some good illustrated Greek MSS.; a few of the miniatures being reproduced in Mrs. Jameson's *Life of Our Lord*, and Canon Farrar's *Life of Christ*.

ones (except the Psalters) are Caedmon's Paraphrase of the Scriptures, in the Bodleian Library at Oxford, and Ælfric's Heptateuch, in the British Museum (Claud. B. iv). The Celtic Gospels only contain miniatures of the Four Evangelists and their symbols, except the *Book of Kells*, at Trinity College, Dublin, which has pictures of the Virgin and Child, the Temptation of Christ, and the Seizure of Christ by the Jews. The best Saxon MSS. containing scenes from the New Testament are: Psalter in the British Museum (Tib. C. vi); the Benedictional of Æthelwold, belonging to the Duke of Devonshire; the great Boulogne Psalter; the Benedictional of Æthelgar, and the Missal of Archbishop Robert, at Rouen. The following Irish MSS. contain scenes from the life of David: Psalter of St. John's College, Cambridge; Psalters in British Museum (Vesp. A. i, and Vit. F. xi).

Illustrations of the miniatures are to be found in the following works:—

Count Bastard, *Peintures et Ornements des Manuscrits, etc., depuis le quatrième siècle, etc.*

J. B. Silvestre, *Paléographie Universel.*

I. O. Westwood, *Palæographia Pictoria Sacra.*

I. O. Westwood, *Miniatures of Anglo-Saxon and Irish MSS.*

Palæographical Society Publications.

Seroux d'Agincourt, *L'Art par les Monuments.*

R. Garrucci, *Storia del Arte Cristiana*, vol. iii.

*Archæologia*, vol. xxiv.

C. Purton Cooper, *Report on Rymer's Fœdera*, Appendix A.

Sir Wm. Betham's *Irish Antiquarian Researches.*

The National MSS. of Ireland.

Dr. J. Stuart, *The Book of Deer.*

Oscar von Gebhart, *Facsimiles of the Ashburnham Pentateuch.*

The illuminated MSS. in the British Museum have been well catalogued by W. de G. Birch and H. Jenner, in their *Early Drawings and Illuminations in the British Museum, with a Dictionary of Subjects*, 1879. A good description of them will be found in Waagen's *Treasures of Art in England.*

# LECTURE II.

## ROMANO-BRITISH PERIOD AND CELTIC SEPULCHRAL MONUMENTS.

ROMANO-BRITISH PERIOD, A.D. 50-400.

AT what time and by whom Christianity was first introduced into this country, will probably never be satisfactorily determined; but there is every reason to believe that a British Church existed nearly three centuries before the landing of Saint Augustine on the shores of Kent in A.D. 597. The earliest historical record that has been preserved concerning pre-Augustinian Christianity in Great Britain is, that in A.D. 314 three bishops were present at the Council held at Arles, in France, to consider the opinions of the Donatists. One came from York, another from the town of London, in the province of York, and the third, either from Lincoln or Caerleon.[1] The British Islands are described as possessing churches and altars by St. Chrysostom, writing A.D. 367; and it is to be inferred, from certain passages in the writings of St. Jerome, that the Britons made pilgrimages to the holy places in Palestine. Pelagius, the author of the Pelagian heresy, at the beginning of the fifth century, concerning man's dependence on the grace of God, was a British Christian whose Greek name was equivalent to Morgan.[2] Gildas, a Welsh monk, who wrote about A.D. 564, asserts that churches existed generally in Britain before the departure of the Romans; and Bede confirms his statements.

Turning from history to archæology, it will be necessary to examine the numerous remains belonging to the period of the

---
[1] Haddan and Stubbs, *Councils, etc.*, vol. i, p. 7.
[2] *Ibid.*, p. 15.

Roman occupation of this country (A.D. 1 to 401), and see whether any distinct traces of Christianity are to be found. It must be admitted that, as a general rule, the explorations of Roman towns, villas, and cemeteries have revealed only objects of a purely pagan type; there are, however, exceptions, as will be seen from the following instances.

In the year 1869, in levelling the ground on the north side of Westminster Abbey, a stone sarcophagus was discovered at a point about 38 ft. from the north wall of the nave, and 46 ft. from the west wall of the north transept. It lay due east and west, and was buried about 2 ft. below the level of the floor of the Abbey, under the remains of some ancient walls. Inside it was found the skeleton of a man, and a few pieces of tile. On one of the long sides of the sarcophagus was an inscription in three lines, as follows:

MEMORIAE . VALER . AMAN
DINI . VALERI . SVPERVEN
TOR . ET   MARCELLVS . PATRI . FECER .

showing that the tomb was made by Superventor and Marcellus for their father, Valerius Amandinus. The inscription is enclosed within a rectangular frame, at each end of which are moon-shaped shield ornaments, similar to those on the sculptured Roman legionary tablet in the Museum of National Antiquities in Edinburgh. The cover of the sarcophagus is a massive block of stone, 7 ft. long and 2 ft. 5 ins. wide, thicker in the middle than at the sides, and having carved upon it a cross in relief, consisting of a long, narrow band running along the central ridge of the cover, and terminating in a head with expanded ends. If it could be proved that this cross was of the same date as the rest of the sarcophagus, it might safely be classed amongst the earliest examples of Christian symbolism in Britain. The character of the ornament on the lower portion of the sarcophagus, and the peculiarities of the lettering (as, for instance, the I extending above the line), show that it is Roman, and probably not later than about the end of the third century.

There is no doubt as to the reading of the inscription, which has been submitted to all the greatest authorities on the subject, both in this country and abroad, and the only point for discussion is as to whether the cross on the cover belongs to the same period as the rest. The chief argument against so early a date as the third century being ascribed to it is, that the use of the cross as a symbol, except in its monogrammatic form, did not become common until the fifth century. Probably one of the first dated examples of the occurrence of the cross is on the sarcophagus of Anicius Probus (A.D. 395), in St. Peter's Church at Rome.[1] It is also to be found on the coins of Galla Placidia[2] (A.D. 425). The lower end of the cross on the Westminster sarcophagus is slightly curved or floriated, which is supposed to indicate a late date. The stone of which both the body of the coffin and the cover are made is the same,—a shelly

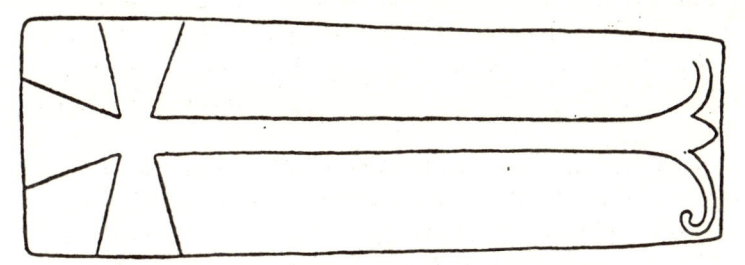

Fig. 1.—Cross on lid of Sarcophagus of Valerius Amandinus.

oolite, such as is found in Oxfordshire. The workmanship of the cover appears to be ruder than that of the rest, and it has been also a good deal damaged by ill-usage. The narrower end of the coffin is carefully bevelled; but the corresponding part of the lid is square.

Shortly after the discovery of the sarcophagus, the late Dean Stanley read a paper on the subject before the British Archæological Institute, and the whole matter was fully discussed[3]; but the opinions expressed differed very widely. The three suppositions to choose from are: (1) that both the body of the sarcophagus and the cover are of the same date, and that

[1] J. W. Appell's *Monuments of Early Christian Art*, p. 12.
[2] *Journ. Brit. Archæolog. Inst.*, vol. xxvii, p. 279.
[3] See papers in *Journ. Brit. Archæol. Inst.*, vol. xxvii, p. 107, by Dean Stanley; p. 110, by Rev. J. McCaul; p. 119, by H. Poole, the Abbey mason; p. 191, by Albert Way; and p. 257, by Rev. J. G. Joyce.

Valerius Amandinus was a Roman Christian, buried probably in the third century; (2) that the sarcophagus and its cover were appropriated by an unknown Christian, perhaps in the fifth or sixth century, at which time the cross was cut; (3) that the sarcophagus only was used at a later date, and an entirely new cover with the Christian symbol added. On the whole, the second supposition seems the most likely.

The sarcophagus is now preserved, in the original state in which it was found, at the entrance of the Chapter House of Westminster Abbey, so that it is open to the inspection of any one wishing to form an opinion on the subject. The dimensions are as follows: outside, 7.0 ft. long, 2 ft. 5 ins. wide at top, and 2 ft.

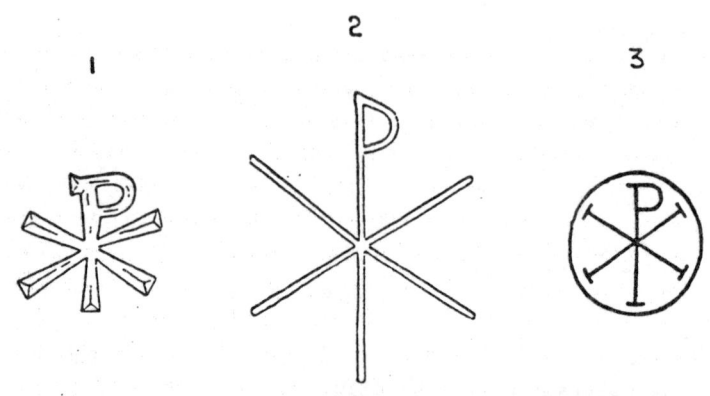

Fig. 2.—The Chi-Rho Monogram from Roman Villas (1 and 2) at Chedworth and (3) at Frampton.

wide at bottom, by 2 ft. 2 ins. deep; inside, 6 ft. $0\frac{1}{4}$ in. long by 1 ft. $7\frac{1}{2}$ ins. wide by 1 ft. 1 in. deep. The cover is 8 ins. thick in the middle and 5 ins. at the sides.

Leaving this rather doubtful example, we next come to what is probably the oldest authentic instance of Christian symbolism of the Romano-British period in Britain. In the year 1794, a very fine Roman pavement was discovered at Frampton, five miles and a half north-west of Dorchester, in Dorsetshire, which was thoroughly explored by the great antiquary, Samuel Lysons.[1] Three rooms and a passage were found to have tesse-

[1] See full illustrations in S. Lysons' *Reliquiæ Britannico Romanæ*, No. 3, pl. 5.

lated floors, the largest of which measured 31 ft. by 21 ft. It was rectangular, with a semicircular apse at one end, and the band of ornament across the apse consisted of a row of seven circles, all filled in with scrolls of foliage, except the centre one, which contained the "Chi-Rho" monogram of Christ. Immediately adjoining was a head of Neptune, with four dolphins on each side, inscribed as follows :

> NEPTVNI VERTEX REGMEN
> SORTITI MOBILE VENTIS
> SCVLTVM CVI CERVLEA EST
> DELFINIS CINCTA DVOBVS.

*The Chi-Rho Monogram.*—The monogram in question consists of a combination of the two Greek letters X and P, which begin the name of Christ (XPICTOC), one placed over the other, so that the vertical stroke of the P cuts the point of intersection of the two cross-strokes of the X. The earliest dated example known on inscriptions from the Catacombs at Rome belongs to the year 331.[1] The origin of the symbol is as follows. On the 6th of the Kalends of November (October 27th), A.D. 312, the Emperor Constantine gained a great victory over his rival Maxentius. We learn from Lactantius,[2] preceptor to the Emperor's eldest son, that on the eve of the encounter "Constantine was admonished in a dream to paint on his soldiers' shields the heavenly sign of God, and so to give battle. He does as he is commanded, and with the letter X placed transversely, having one extremity bent round, he marks their shields with Christ. Armed with this sign his army draws the sword." The next day, after conquering under the sign of the cross, Constantine entered Rome in triumph, and summoning artists, commanded them to make the labarum, or standard, of which Eusebius[3] gives the following description. "It was a long spear, gilt and provided with a transverse bar like a cross. Above, at the top of this same spear, was fixed a wreath of gold and precious stones. In the centre of the wreath was

---

[1] Northcote's *Epitaphs of the Catacombs*, p. 30. Martigny, in his *Dict. des Ant. Chrét.*, p. 478, mentions an earlier example dated A.D. 323, discovered recently.

[2] *De Mort. Persec.*, c. 44.

[3] *Vit. Constant.*, lib i, c. 31.

the sign of the saving name (of Jesus Christ); that is to say, a monogram setting forth this holy name by its first two letters combined, the P in the middle of the X. These same letters the Emperor was accustomed henceforth to wear on his helmet. Now to the cross-bar of the labarum which cuts the spear obliquely was hung a kind of veil, or purple fabric, enriched with precious stones, artistically combined with each other, and which dazzled the eyes by their splendour, and with gold embroidery of indescribable beauty. This veil fixed to the cross-bar was as broad as it was long, and had on the upper part of it the bust of the Emperor beloved by God and his children, embroidered in gold, or rather perhaps their medals in gold, hung beneath the banner. The Emperor always used this safe standard as a protecting sign of the power of God against his enemies, and caused ensigns made after the same pattern to be carried with all his armies." This standard occurs on the coins of Constantine,[1] and is to be seen on one of the sarcophagi at the Vatican, with the words of the Emperor's dream, EN TOTTΩ NIKA ("Under this thou shalt conquer") inscribed upon it.[2]

The use of the Chi-Rho monogram of Christ soon spread from Rome to other countries, and it is found on monuments in France between the years A.D. 377 and 340.[3] The date of the Frampton pavement must lie between A.D. 312, when the monogram was first introduced, and A.D. 401, when the Roman occupation of Britain ceased. Two other Roman pavements found in this country may possibly be Christian,—that at Harpole,[4] in Northamptonshire, which has in the centre a circle divided into eight parts by radial lines, so as to resemble one form of the monogram; and that at Horkstow Hall,[5] in Lincolnshire, which has some small red crosses amongst the decorations. The Christian monogram is carved twice upon a stone forming the under part of the foundation of the steps leading

---

[1] Martigny's *Dict. Ant. Chrét.*, p. 520; and King's *Early Christian Numismatics*.
[2] Martigny's *Dict.*, p. 404.
[3] Ed. Le Blant, *Inscr. Chrét. de la Gaule*.
[4] *Journ. Brit. Archæol. Assoc.*, vol. vi, p. 126.
[5] S. Lysons' *Reliquiæ Britannico Romanæ*, pl. 3.

into the corridor of the Roman villa at Chedworth,[1] in Gloucestershire. (Fig. 2.)

It appears, then, that the number of sepulchral remains and structures belonging to the period of the Roman occupation, which show any trace of the existence of Christianity, is infinitesimally small; and the same may be said with regard to the objects discovered in connection with them, the following being a list of the examples at present known:—A silver bowl, found at Corbridge,[2] in Northumberland, and now lost, having upon it the Christian monogram repeated six times; two oval cakes of pewter, found in the Thames near Battersea, and now in the British Museum,[3] one stamped with the monogram and the word SPES, and the other with the monogram and the Alpha and Omega repeated twice; a fragment of a metal foot-rule, in the York Museum,[4] marked with the monogram; a piece of Samian ware found at Catterick Bridge,[5] in Yorkshire, belonging to Sir Wilfrid Lawson, with a cross upon it, perhaps Christian; a terra-cotta lamp in the Museum at Newcastle-on-Tyne,[6] with the monogram.

The very small number of Roman objects ornamented with Christian devices, as compared with the total quantity of antiquities discovered in Great Britain, tends to show that Christianity can have made but little progress here during the first four centuries.

### Celtic Sepulchral Monuments (a.d. 400-1066).

The next class of remains to which we shall turn our attention are those which show no trace of Roman influence, but yet bear witness to the existence of an early Celtic Church in this country before the landing of St. Augustine. There are certain peculiarities of ritual, of ecclesiastical observances, of architecture, and of the texts, lettering, and ornamentation of the

---

[1] *Journ. Brit. Archæol. Assoc.*, vol. xxiii, p. 228.
[2] Gough's *Camden*, vol. iii, p. 509.
[3] *Journ. Brit. Achæol. Inst.*, vol. xvi, p. 88; and vol. xxiii, p. 68.
[4] C. Wellbeloved's *Handbook of the Antiquities in the York Museum* (7th edition, 1881), p. 114.
[5] *Journ. Brit. Archæol. Inst.*, vol. vi, p. 81.
[6] Hübner's *Inscr. Brit. Christ.*, p. 81.

MSS., which show that the Celtic Church had an origin earlier and entirely independent of the Roman form of Christianity introduced by St. Augustine. The two chief points of difference which existed between the observances of the Roman and Celtic Churches previous to the Synod of Whitby in A.D. 664 were the time of keeping Easter and the method of tonsure.

The Celtic calculation of Easter corresponded with that of the Roman Church before the Council of Nice (A.D. 325), when the new fashion was introduced, the reason for the change being astronomical, and not theological.[1] The Celtic Church, which was isolated from the rest of Christendom, still adhered to the old calculation, until, in the seventh century, the matter became one of crucial controversy at the Synod of Whitby, between Colman, on the side of the Scots, and Wilfrid, on the side of Rome, and was decided finally in favour of the latter, the Celts agreeing to conform to the Roman usage.[2] On the statue of St. Hippolytus, of the third century, in the Lateran Museum at Rome, is inscribed his Paschal canon.[3]

The difference between the Roman and the Celtic tonsure was, that in the former case the crown of the head was shaved in a circle, whereas in the latter the whole of the hair in front of a line drawn over the top of the head from ear to ear was removed.[4] There were also other differences, as regards the rite of baptism, the ordination of bishops, and the consecration of churches, which need not occupy our attention here.

The characteristics of the architecture of the Celtic Church have been treated of in a previous course of Rhind Lectures,[5] and the peculiarities of the texts and the palæography of the MSS. will be found fully described in the works of Professor I. O. Westwood.[6]

The earliest historical fact recorded about Christianity in Ireland is by Prosper Aquitanus, who describes the mission sent

---

[1] F. E. Warren's *Liturgy and Ritual of the Celtic Church*, p. 64 ; Rev. G. F. Browne's *Venerable Bede*, p. 51.

[2] Bede's *Eccl. Hist.*, book III, chap. 25.

[3] Northcote and Brownlow's *Roma Sotterranea*, vol. ii, p. 263.

[4] Warren's *Liturgy of the Celtic Church*, p. 67 ; Bede's *Eccl. Hist.*, book v, chap. 21.

[5] *Scotland in Early Christian Times*, 1st Series.

[6] *Palæographia Pictoria Sacra;* and *Miniatures of Celtic and Anglo-Saxon MSS.*

in A.D. 431, to "the Scots believing in Christ".[1] This mission seems to have proved abortive, and led to nothing more than the baptising of a few converts and the erection of three wooden churches.[2] The real Christianising of Ireland is, however, undoubtedly due to St. Patrick, who is supposed to have been born about A.D. 387, and probably landed in Ireland in A.D. 440. His death is recorded in the *Annals of the Four Masters* under the year A.D. 493.[3]

There was an intimate connection in early times between the Celtic churches of Gaul and Britain, as is shown by the presence of British bishops, attested by their signatures, between A.D. 461 and A.D. 555,[4] and the visit of Germanus, Bishop of Auxerre, and Lupus, Bishop of Troyes, in A.D. 429,[5] to confute the Pelagians at Verulamium. Many of the Celtic churches are dedicated to Gallican saints,—as, for example, the very ancient ones at Canterbury, and Whithorne in Wigtonshire, to St. Martin of Tours; others in Cornwall and Wales to St. Germanus of Auxerre; and in Glamorganshire to St. Hilary of Arles, and St. Lupus of Troyes (under the name of St. Bleddian).[6] "The British Church employed the Paschal cycle of Gaul as drawn up by Sulpicius Severus, the disciple of St. Martin (*circa* A.D. 410), whilst the Irish Church followed the still earlier cycle of Anatolius. The Gallican Psalter, or the second revision made by St. Jerome, A.D. 387-391, was also used by the British Church."[7]

There are traces also of a connection between the Spanish and Celtic Churches (A.D. 380 to 693), indicated by the signatures of British bishops who were present at Spanish Councils, by the existence of the British method of calculating Easter, and by the tonsure.[8]

---

[1] Haddan and Stubbs' *Councils, etc.*, vol. ii, p. 290.
[2] *Annals of the Four Masters*, i, 129.
[3] Haddan and Stubbs' *Councils, etc.*, vol. ii, p. 295.
[4] Warren's *Liturgy of the Celtic Church*, p. 59.
[5] Haddan and Stubbs' *Councils, etc.*, vol. i, p. 16.
[6] Rees' *Welsh Saints*, p. 126; and Haddan and Stubbs' *Councils, etc.*, vol. ii, p. 86.
[7] Warren's *Liturgy of the Celtic Church*, p. 60.
[8] Warren's *Liturgy of the Celtic Church*, p. 62; Haddan and Stubbs' *Councils, etc.*, vol. ii, p. 99.

Whatever similarities then existed between the Celtic and Eastern Churches in matters of observance, and in the symbolism and ornamentation of the MSS. and sculptured stones, are to be explained, not by there having been a direct intercourse between Britain and the East, but by the connection with the Gallic Church at a time when Eastern influence affected the whole of Christendom.[1]

The early Celtic saint was essentially a celibate and a hermit, choosing the wildest and most inaccessible places,[2] in order that he might devote himself to a life of seclusion and self-denial, and to the founding of those monastic schools[3] which became in time the great centres of learning and missionary enterprise throughout the country. Foremost amongst such men in Gaul was St. Martin of Tours, who was born about A.D. 316 and died in A.D. 400. The school which he established in the west of France led directly to the Christianising of parts of Britain which had before been pagan; for at the beginning of the fifth century (A.D. 410 to 432), St. Ninian, after visiting St. Martin at Tours, landed in Scotland, and at Whithorne in Wigtonshire (*Ad Candidam Casam*) built a church of stone, after a fashion unusual amongst the Britons,[4] and dedicated it to St. Martin. This was the first attempt to convert the Southern Picts, but the Christianising of the rest of Scotland did not begin until about 150 years later, when St. Columba came to Scotland from Ireland, in A.D. 563.[5]

Northumbria received its Christianity indirectly from Ireland through Iona, when Aidan was made first Bishop of Lindisfarne by King Oswald[6] in A.D. 635.

Our knowledge of the early Welsh saints is derived chiefly from lives written in the twelfth century. St. Dubricius, the first bishop of Llandaff, lived at the end of the sixth century (A.D. 550-600), and his successor, St. Teilo, together with St.

---

[1] See Warren's *Liturgy of the Celtic Church*, p. 46.

[2] Hence the frequent occurrence of the name Dysart, or *desertum*, in Ireland and Scotland.

[3] The name Bangor was given to several of these schools, and places in Wales and Ireland still retain the title.

[4] Bede's *Eccl. Hist.*, bk. III, chap. 4.

[5] Haddan and Stubbs.

[6] Bede's *Eccl. Hist.*, bk. III, chap. 3.

Padarn and St. Cybi, were contemporaries of St. David, who died A.D. 601. St. Cadoc, who founded the monastery of Llancarvan in Glamorganshire, and who was educated at Lismore in Ireland, was present at the Synod of Llandewi Brefi, in A.D. 569. St. Iltutus was born in Brittany, and his name is associated with Llantwit Major in Glamorganshire. He was the founder of the college at Caerworgen, in the diocese of Llandaff, where St. David, St. Samson of Dol, Paulinus, and Gildas are supposed to have been educated, so that he must have lived at the beginning of the sixth century.[1]

The duration of the Celtic Church in Britain was as follows. In Central England it became extinct about the end of the fifth century, owing to the Saxon invasions; the Welsh conformed to the usages of the Anglo-Saxon Church at the end of the eighth century, but the supremacy of the see of Canterbury was not fully established until the twelfth century; the British Church in Cornwall became subject to the see of Canterbury in the time of King Athelstan (A.D. 925-940); the Celtic Church established in Northumberland by King Oswald conformed to the Roman usage after the Synod of Whitby in A.D. 664; the Britons of Strathclyde conformed in A.D. 688, and the Church of Iona in A.D. 772; but customs peculiar to the ancient Church survived until the eleventh century.[2]

From the above historical evidence, which has been gone into somewhat at length, it appears that the extreme limits of the duration of the Celtic Church, which originated in Gaul, and thence spread to Brittany, Ireland, Wales, Scotland, and the North of England, are from about the year A.D. 400 to 1100.

We shall now proceed to examine the objects and monuments belonging to this period which show traces of Christian symbolism. The early Celtic ecclesiastical buildings which have survived to the present time are exceedingly plain and simple, and have no ornamental features of any kind; but some of the later round towers and churches have sculpture used sparingly over the doorways, which will be described hereafter. A few specimens of Christian Celtic metal-work, such as shrines for books, bells, or relics, croziers, chalices, and processional crosses,

---

[1] See *Haddan and Stubbs*, vol. i; and Rees' *Welsh Saints*.
[2] *Warren*, p. 1.

have symbolical subjects upon them. Our knowledge of Celtic Christian symbolism is, however, derived almost entirely from the study of the sepulchral monuments and sculptured stones.

It may be worth while remarking that no other nation possesses such a wonderful series of monuments, illustrating the history of Christian art at one of its most obscure periods, and probably no other nation would have treated them with such scorn, or allowed them to be so ruthlessly destroyed. Many of these priceless treasures have been lost altogether, others have been damaged by persons ignorant of their real value, and the whole are perishing miserably from exposure to the weather. Casts, or at least photographs, should be taken before every trace of the sculpture has disappeared. This is the more important, as many fragments, which have been preserved for centuries by being built into the walls of churches, are being brought to light from time to time in the course of modern restorations and alterations, and these are now also in many cases exposed to the weather. A gallery of casts of Celtic sculptured stones would be invaluable for purposes of archæological research, and might be the means of reviving the national taste for the art of sculpture, in which our own countrymen at one time attained so high a standard of excellence.

The Celtic monuments of the Christian period are divided into two distinct classes.

1. *Rude Pillar-stones*—rough, unhewn monoliths, erect, with incised crosses, sometimes accompanied by an inscription in debased Latin capitals or in Oghams.

2. *Sculptured Stones*—with the characteristic forms of Celtic ornament and figure-subjects cut in relief, upon stones carefully dressed and shaped either into the form of a cross, a sepulchral slab, or a recumbent coped stone; sometimes accompanied by an inscription in Irish minuscules, in Saxon uncials, or in Scandinavian Runes.

The chief peculiarities of the rude pillar-stones are: (1) the stone being used in its natural state, without any attempt at dressing or squaring. Long pieces of hard volcanic rock were generally chosen, not often exceeding 6 ft. in length, and they were placed upright in a hole dug in the ground, there being no socket-stone or base of any kind; (2) the absence of ornamental features; (3) the cross being incised, and of the simplest form, generally consisting either of two lines crossing at right angles, or a cross patée, within a circle; (4) the inscription, which is cut vertically up the face of the stone, being in debased Latin capitals and in the Latin language, with the name of the deceased, and the formula "*hic jacet*"; or in Ogham characters, and the name of the deceased with the word "*maqui*" (son of), in the Celtic language. In some cases the inscriptions are biliteral and bilingual.

The geographical distribution of rude pillar-stones is as follows. In Ireland there are 121; in Wales 107; in Devon and Cornwall 30; and in Scotland only five. In England they are unknown, except in the two western counties mentioned. It seems clear, therefore, that Ireland was the chief centre from which this class of monument originated, and their absence in Central England points to their date being post-Roman.

The actual date of the erection of any of the rude pillar-stones has not been ascertained; for although almost all the inscriptions contain proper names, none of them have been identified with characters known in history, which alone tends to show the great age of these monuments. It is tolerably certain that they belong to the transition period between Christianity and paganism, as they are only found either in connection with semi-pagan remains, or upon the earliest Christian sites. The absence of dressing or ornament, the archaic forms of the lettering, the names and the language, together with the frequent use of the formula "*hic jacet*", which occurs on Christian inscriptions in the Catacombs at Rome, all show that the rude pillar-stones are older than the sculptured crosses with Celtic forms of ornament.

The chief characteristics of the later sculptured crosses are entirely different from those of the rude pillar-stones, and are as follows: (1) That the stone is carefully dressed and cut out into the shape it is intended to assume, either of an erect cross, or an erect cross-slab, or a cylindrical pillar, or a recumbent cross-slab, or a coped tombstone. The crosses are sometimes made of several pieces morticed together, and are generally fixed firmly in a stone socket at the base; (2) that there is a profusion of those kinds of ornament which are peculiar to Celtic art, such as interlaced-work, key and spiral patterns, and conventional animals, with their bodies, limbs, and tails interlaced, the design being divided up into panels, each of which is complete in itself, and is enclosed in a frame composed of a flat band, roll, or cable moulding; (3) that the inscriptions are cut in horizontal lines across the stone, and that formulæ are more varied, being generally to the effect that " A. erected this cross to B. Pray for his soul"; (4) that the language and lettering differs according to the locality, the language being either Latin, Celtic, or Scandinavian, and the letters Irish minuscules and Saxon uncials (corresponding with those in the MSS. of the same period), or the Runes of Northern Europe. In Scotland a few sculptured stones with Celtic ornament and Ogham inscriptions occur; but these are exceptional. The dates of many of the later sculptured stones have been satisfactorily determined by means of the names mentioned in the inscriptions, which have been identified with historical personages.

The most reliable evidence as to the age of sculptured stones with Celtic ornament is derived from the series of 179 sepulchral cross-slabs at Clonmacnois in Ireland,[1] eighty-one of which have been dated, by means of the names inscribed, between the years A.D. 628 and 1273. Out of these, only sixty-seven have any ornament besides the cross, thirty-two being dated by means of the names inscribed. The earliest slab with ornament is the tombstone of Tuathgal,[2] Abbot of Clonmacnois, A.D. 806. The tombstone of Suibine,[3] the scribe of Clonmacnois (A.D. 887), of St. Fiacraich[4] (A.D. 921), and of St. Berechtuire[5] at Tullylease (A.D. 839), are elaborate specimens of Celtic ornament, and there is no doubt whatever either as to the identity of the persons or the date. Of the free standing high crosses of Ireland, which are very ornate, five are dated by means of inscriptions containing historical names, namely, those at Monasterboice (A.D. 924); Clonmacnois (A.D. 914), and the two at Tuam (A.D. 1106).[6] Two of the Welsh inscribed and sculptured stones at Llantwit Major in Glamorganshire, set up to the memory of Samson and to Howel ap Rhys, are, from historical and palæographical

---

[1] Petrie's *Irish Inscriptions*, vol. i, p. 13.
[2] *Ibid.*, pl. xii, No. 29.
[3] *Ibid.*, pl. xxxi, No. 82.
[4] *Ibid.*, pl. xxxvii, No. 95.
[5] *Ibid.*, vol. ii, pl. xxx, No. 64.
[6] *Ibid.*, p. 151.

evidence, ascribed by Prof I. O. Westwood to the close of the ninth century (A.D. 843-884). The inscribed cross at St. Vigeans in Forfarshire is of similar character, and probably belongs to the same period. The evidence as to the age of the sculptured stones of Northumbria is rather unreliable. Professor Stephens considers the crosses at Bewcastle, Collingham, and Ruthwell to have been erected in the seventh century. The cross at Hackness in Yorkshire is the oldest with a satisfactory date (A.D. 705-773). The crosses of the Isle of Man belong to the period of the Scandinavian occupation (A.D. 888 to 1226), as is proved by their Runic inscriptions.[1]

The general result of the above investigation is to show that in Ireland, where Celtic art originated, none of the ornamented sculptured stones can be proved to be older than the ninth century, and therefore it is very improbable that those in England, Scotland, and Wales can be ascribed to an earlier period. There is consequently a gap of about 400 years which has to be accounted for, between the first introduction of Christianity into Ireland, and the time when sculptured crosses began to be erected. What are the monuments belonging to this earlier period? The rude pillar-stones supply the obvious answer to the question, and we shall now proceed to examine their symbolism.

### Rude Pillar Stones (A.D. 402-700).

Most of the rude pillar-stones with Christian symbols are inscribed, but there are others with simple incised crosses carved upon them, having no lettering whatever. At the outset we are met with difficulties concerning both these classes of monuments. As regards the former, it is not always possible to say with any degree of certainty whether the cross and the inscription were cut at the same time. The late Mr. Rolt Brash, in his *Inscribed Monuments of the Gaedhil*, looks upon most of the Ogham inscriptions as of pagan origin, and considers that the stones on which they were cut were appropriated at a subsequent period for Christian gravestones, when the cross was added. It will be seen, however, on examination, that most of the crosses referred to are of the simplest and earliest form, and

[1] Cumming's *Runic Remains of the Isle of Man.*

there seems no reason to doubt that a large proportion at all events are coeval with the inscriptions. With regard to those rude pillar-stones which have crosses, but are without letters, there is often no means of determining the age, as a simple form of cross may be of any date.

There are only three Christian symbols which occur on the rude pillar-stones, namely, the Chi-Rho monogram, the cross, and the Alpha and Omega.

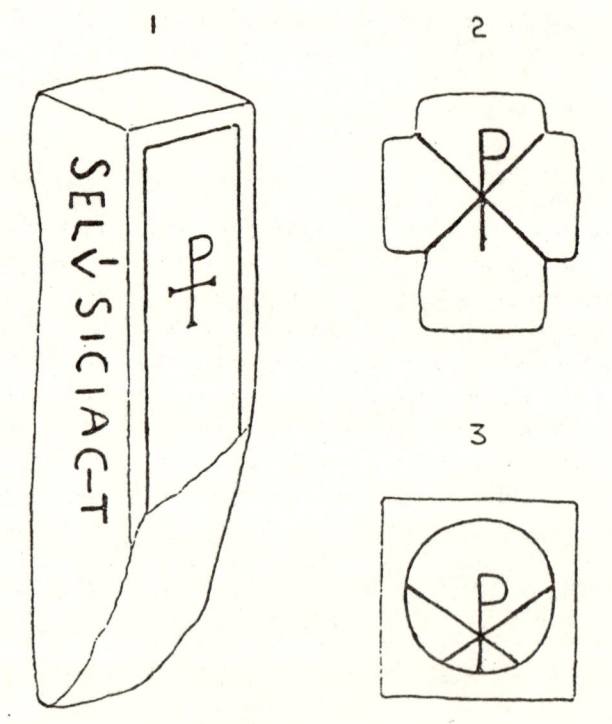

Fig. 3.—The Chi-Rho Monogram on Stones in Cornwall—(1) at St. Just, (2) at St. Helen's Chapel, (3) at Phillack.

*The Chi-Rho Monogram and the Cross.*—Very few examples of the existence of the Christian monogram on stone monuments are known in Great Britain, there being three in the west of England, one in North Wales, four in the south-west of Scotland, and none in Ireland. Those in Cornwall are as follows: In the chancel of St. Just in Penwith Church is preserved a small stone, which was found in a watercourse near the ruins of St. Helen's Chapel, Cape Cornwall.[1] It measures 11 inches by 9 inches,[2] and is cut out rudely into the form of a cross, on the face of which is carved the Chi-Rho monogram of the most common shape, that is to say, X and P combined. A similar monogram, but enclosed in a circle five inches in diameter, is to be seen upon a small stone built into the wall of the porch

Fig. 4.—Chi-Rho Monogram on Stone at Penmachno.

of Phillack Church, above the doorway, which was found when the church was rebuilt in 1856.[3] The third Cornish stone is now deposited in the chancel of the Church of St. Just in Penwith, where it was discovered during the rebuilding in 1834.[4]

[1] J. T. Blight's *Crosses of Cornwall*, 3rd ed., p. 61.
[2] *Journ. Brit. Archæol. Inst.*, vol. iv, p. 304.
[3] *Archæologia Cambrensis*, 1858, p. 181.
[4] *Journ. Brit. Archæol. Inst.*, vol. iv, p. 303.

It measures 3 feet 6 inches long by 1 foot 2 inches wide by 9 inches thick. On the edge is an inscription in debased Latin characters—

SENILVS IC JACIT

and on the adjoining face is the monogram in its later form, consisting of the P with a horizontal cross-stroke.

The Welsh example is of the same shape, and is to be found on a stone in Penmachno Church, Caernarvonshire.[1] The slab measures 1 foot 10 inches long by 11 inches wide, and the monogram is placed above the inscription, which is in debased Latin capitals, to the following effect:

CARAVSIVS HIC JACIT IN HOC CONGERIES LAPIDVM.

In Scotland the geographical area in which the stones with the monogram exist is confined to the two most southern promontories of Wigtonshire. In the old burying-ground of Kirkmadrine, in the parish of Stoneykirk, are two blocks of whinstone, about 5 feet high and 1 foot 6 inches broad, used at present as gateposts.[2] One has an inscription in Latin capitals—

HIC IACENT SCI ET PRÆCIPVI SACERDOTES ID EST VIVENTIVS ET MAVORIVS.

("Here lie the holy and excellent priests, to wit, Viventius and Mavorius.") Above the inscription is a circle enclosing a cross, the upper limb of which is bent round like the letter R. This is a form of the Chi-Rho monogram having a special interest, as it shows the way in which the early crosses were developed out of the monogram. Above are the Alpha and Omega.

The other stone at Kirkmadrine has the same type of monogram, but without the Alpha and Omega. It is inscribed

.. S ET FLORENTIVS.

A drawing of a third stone, with the monogram just like the preceding, and inscribed

INITIVM ET FINIS,

has been preserved by Dr. A. Mitchell, in the *Proceedings* of

---

[1] I. O. Westwood's *Lapidarium Walliæ*, pl. 79, No. 2, and p. 175; *Archæologia Cambrensis*, 1863, p. 257.

[2] *Proc. Soc. Ant. Scot.*, vol. ix, p. 568; Stuart's *Sculptured Stones*, vol. ii, pl. 71.

the Society of Antiquaries of Scotland; but the monument itself is unfortunately either lost or destroyed..

On the high ground above the town of Whithorne, on the side of the road leading to the Isle of Whithorne, stands a stone slab

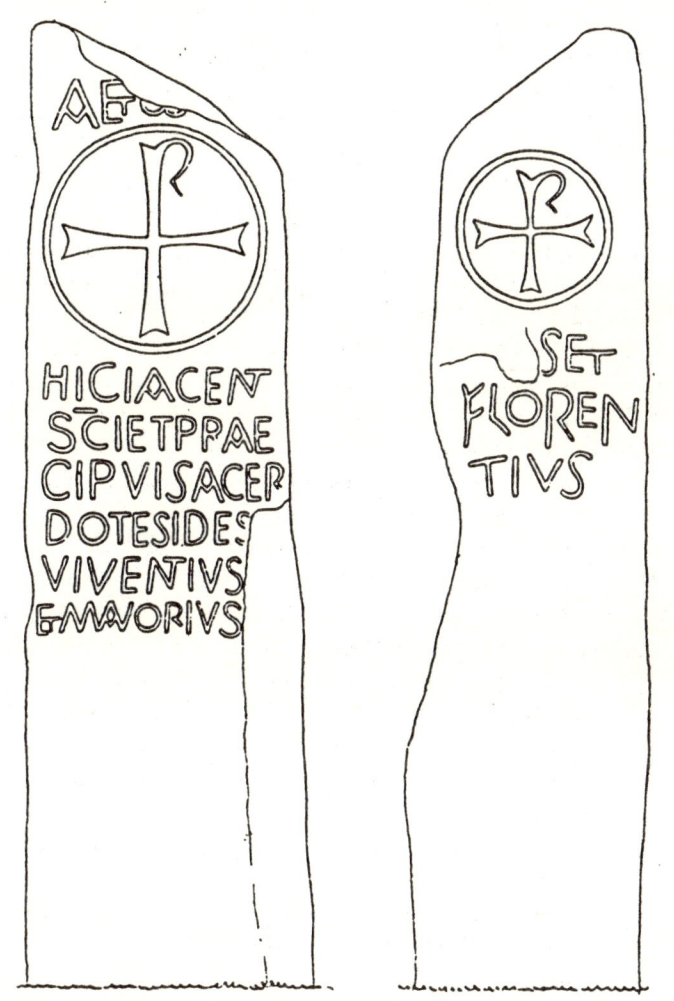

Fig. 5.—Chi-Rho Monogram on Stones at Kirkmadrine.

about 4 ft. high and 2 ft. broad.¹ Its original site is unknown. It has on the face an inscription in Latin capitals—

LOCI (S)TI PETRI APVSTOLI,

¹ *Proc. Soc. Ant. Scot.*, vol. ix, p. 578; Stuart's *Sculptured Stones*, vol. ii, pl. 78.

and, above, an incised cross with expanded ends of the Maltese pattern within a double circular line. It has a lower limb attached at the bottom, and at the right-hand upper corner is the termination like the letter R, showing that it is intended for the Chi-Rho monogram. This is probably one of the oldest memorials of Christianity in Scotland, and belongs to the time when, as Bede tells us, "the Southern Picts relinquished the error of idolatry and received the true faith, by the preaching of the word to them, by Bishop Nynias, a most reverend and holy man, of the nation of the Britons, who had been regularly taught at Rome the faith and mysteries of the truth, whose episcopal see, remarkable for a church dedicated to St. Martin, the Bishop (of Tours), where he himself, together with more Saints, rests in the body, is now in the possession of the nation of the Angles. Which place belongs to the province of the Bernicii, and is commonly called Ad Candidam Casam, because he had there built a Church of stone, after a fashion unusual among the Britons."[1]

Fig. 6.—Combined Cross and Monogram on Stone at Whithorne.

The Ad Candidam Casam of Bede has been identified with Whithorne, and "in a letter of James V, to Pope Innocent X, he says that the tomb of Ninian was still to be seen there, and that pilgrims from England,

[1] Bede, *Eccl. Hist.*, bk. III, chap. 4.

Ireland, the Isles, and adjoining countries, yearly flocked to pay their devotions at his shrine."[1]

The various forms of the Chi-Rho monogram, just described, illustrate the changes and developments which took place in the symbol from the time of Constantine (A.D. 312), when it was a simple combination of the two Greek letters X and P, to the sixth century, when it became a cross within a circle. The origin of the monogram must be referred to Constantine's dream, previously mentioned, with regard to which the historian Gibbon

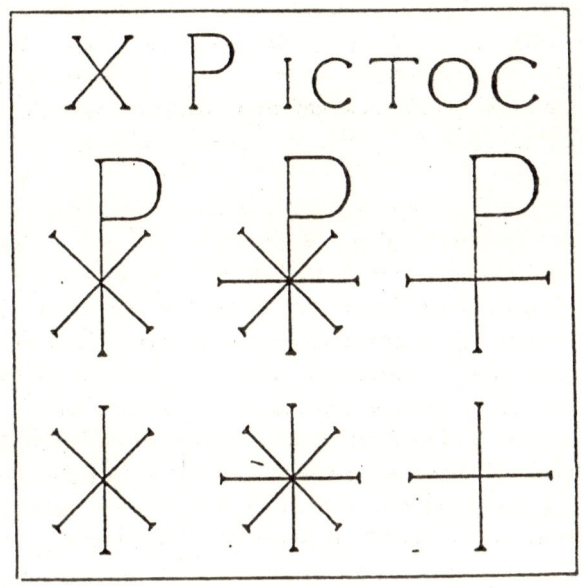

Fig. 7.—Various forms of the Chi Rho Monogram.

has expressed so much incredulity. It is not to be supposed that Constantine invented the symbol, for it is found on coins many centuries before his time; but whereas there are hardly any examples of its occurrence on Christian monuments before A.D. 323,[2] after that time it was universally recognised as signifying the name of the Saviour, and used on coins, memorial inscriptions, sarcophagi, mosaics, lamps, glass vessels, and, in fact, throughout the whole range of sacred art.

[1] Stuart's *Sculptured Stones*, vol. ii, p. 52.

[2] Earliest known instance found under the pavement of Basilica of St. Laurence, in agro Verano (A.D. 323). See Martigny's *Dict.*, p. 478.

The most ancient form of the monogram was in all probability that in which an x is made on the down-stroke of the P; but the other one, where a horizontal cross-bar is substituted for the x, was introduced soon after, for it is found also on the coins of Constantine. The accidental resemblance of the Greek letter x to the cross of the Passion gives a reason why the monogram should have become such a favourite symbol, and also explains the changes which took place in its shape. All the different variations can be traced to two causes—(1) the addition of a horizontal cross-stroke to the original form; and (2) the gradual alteration in the shape of the top of the P, which became more like an R, and finally the little tail was dropped altogether. Thus the P with the horizontal cross-stroke was obtained, first, by adding an additional horizontal bar to the original monogram, and then dropping the x. The cross-forms, consisting either of an I and x combined, or a + and x, result from the omission of the top of the P. Two or three of the variations often occur together on the same coin, or sarcophagus, showing that there was a good deal of caprice in the choice of forms, and that no special one was adhered to rigidly. The addition of the letters Alpha and Omega took place as early as A.D. 347,[1] and the monogram is found enclosed in a circle in A.D. 339.[2] The Alpha and Omega are generally placed at each side of the x in the first kind of monogram, and below the cross-bar in the second kind, being often hung by chains to it. The origin of the circle is either ornamental, or may be taken from the circular wreath or crown of glory within which the monogram is so often inscribed. The idea of eternity is also associated with the circle, as is seen from an inscription found at Milan[3]:

"Circulus hic summi comprehendit nomini regis
Quem sine principio et sine fine vides."

The circle of the monogram survives in the ring which joins the arms of the Celtic crosses. The period during which the

---

[1] Martigny's *Dict.*, p. 478; Northcote, in his *Epitaphs of the Catacombs*, gives A.D. 362. The Alpha and Omega occurs on the coins of Constantius (*Martigny*, p. 522).

[2] De Rossi, *Christian Inscr. of Rome*, No. 339.

[3] *Scotland in Early Christian Times*, 2nd Series, p. 252.

monogram was most frequently used, was that of the sculptured sarcophagi at Rome, from the fourth to the sixth centuries. On the sarcophagi it occupies a central position in the design, which is arranged symmetrically on each side of it. Sometimes it is placed between a pair of doves, or peacocks, or lambs, or it appears on the summit of a cross, with soldiers below. When used in epitaphs, it is either placed at the top, in the middle, as a symbol, or has such words as " in signo", or merely " in", prefixed. A curious instance of the introduction of the monogram

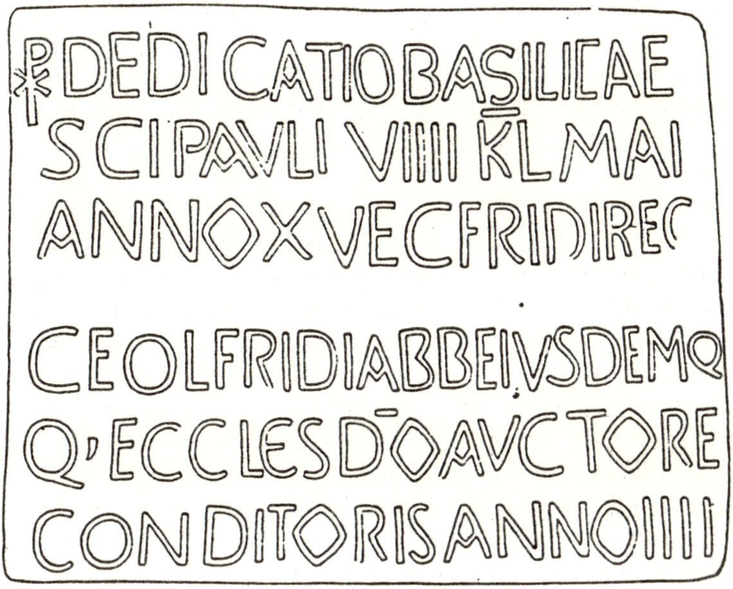

℟ DEDICATIO BASILICAE
SCI PAVLI VIIII KL MAI
ANNO XV ECFRIDIREC
CEOLFRIDI ABBEIVSDEMQ
Q' ECCLES D̄O AVCTORE
CONDITORIS ANNO IIII

Fig. 8.—Chi-Rho Monogram on Dedication Stone at Jarrow.

in the middle of an inscription is on a stone at Trawsfynydd in Merionethshire, North Wales.[1]

    PORIVS HIC IN TVMVLO JACIT
    HOMO X̄PIANVS FVIT.

Here the monogram forms the beginning of the word CHRISTIANVS, and is of a remarkable shape, like a P with a C placed together.

The period over which the use of the monogram extends

[1] Westwood's *Lapidarium Walliæ*, pl. 77, No. 7, p. 161.

in Gaul, as shown by dated inscriptions, is from A.D. 377 to 493.[1] Its use, however, lasted longer in this country, as there is an instance at the beginning of the inscription on the dedication stone of the church at Jarrow,[2] in the county of Durham, which was dedicated to St. Paul, in the fifteenth year of the reign of Ecfrid, King of Northumbria (or A.D. 685).

The monograms on the pillars at Kirkmadrine bear a great resemblance to those sculptured over the doorways of houses in Syria, of the sixth century, which have been illustrated in

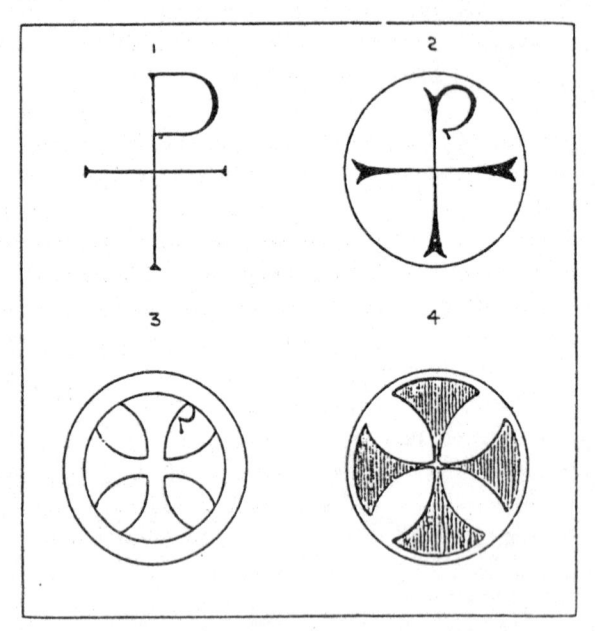

Fig. 9.—Development of Cross out of Monogram on Stones (1) at Penmachno, (2) Kirkmadrine, (3) Whithorne, (4) Aglish.

C. J. M. de Vogüé's magnificent work on the subject.[3] The bars composing the monogram have expanded ends, and intersect at right angles in the centre of the enclosing circle; the loop of the P is now little more than the curving over of the upper end of the vertical bar, and when this disappears we get

[1] Le Blant, *Inscr. Chrét. de la Gaule*, vol. i, p. 12.
[2] Hübner's *Christian Inscr.*, No. 198.
[3] *Syrie Centrale—Architecture Civile et Religieuse.* Some illustrations reproduced by Martigny, p. 481.

the simple Maltese cross, which is found on some of the Ogham inscribed and other rude pillar-stones of the earlier Celtic Christian period. To these we shall now direct our attention.

Out of about 258 rude pillar-stones with Ogham and debased Latin inscriptions, in Great Britain, there are some thirty which have crosses in addition. The question of whether the crosses are of the same date as the inscriptions, or whether the Christian symbol was a later addition, is one on which there exists a considerable divergence of opinion. Unless, however, it can be shown, either that the form of the cross is one which is unknown at so early a period, or that it has ornamental peculiarities of a late character, or that it is cut in such a way as to interfere with the inscription, there is no reason to doubt that both the cross and the inscription were executed at the same time,—although, of course, there is no possible means of proving that such is the case. Out of all the examples which have been engraved by Brash and Westwood, in their works on the subject,[1] there is only one instance where the cross destroys the inscription.[2] The cross is generally of the simplest and most ancient form, and incised, without ornament of any kind.

In Ireland the monuments in question are in many instances found on sites associated with the names of early saints, or in what were formerly Christian graveyards, but are used now only for burying unbaptised infants, and persons who have committed suicide. One of the oldest forms of the cross is that known as the Maltese within a circle. It is the same as that on the Whithorne stone, but without any trace of the monogram. There are four examples of rude pillar-stones on which this type of cross occurs :—three in the county of Kerry in Ireland,[3] and one in Pembrokeshire, South Wales,[4] all with Ogham inscriptions. Perhaps the most remarkable is that at Aglish, in the county of Kerry, which has, in addition to a Maltese cross within a circle, two small Buddhist crosses, or

---

[1] *Ogham Monuments of the Gaedhil*, and Westwood's *Lapidarium Walliæ*.

[2] At Silion, Cardiganshire; *Westwood*, pl. 66, No. 1.

[3] Maumenorig, Aglish, Brandon Mountain. (*Brash*, pls. 21, 24, 27.)

[4] Dugoed, near Clydai. (*Westwood*, pl. 59.)

Swasticas, on each side of an equilateral triangle. The Swastica, although originally a pagan symbol found on early Greek coins and pottery, and on the feet of Buddha, was adopted at an early period by the Christians, and is to be seen on the paintings of Diogenes Fossor[1] and the Good Shepherd,[2] of the fourth century, in the Catacombs at Rome. It is found on the Newton stone in Aberdeenshire,[3] on a stone at Craigentarget, Glenluce,[4] and on three sepulchral slabs in Ireland.[5] In later times the Swastica appears chiefly on ecclesiastical vestments, sepulchral brasses,[6]

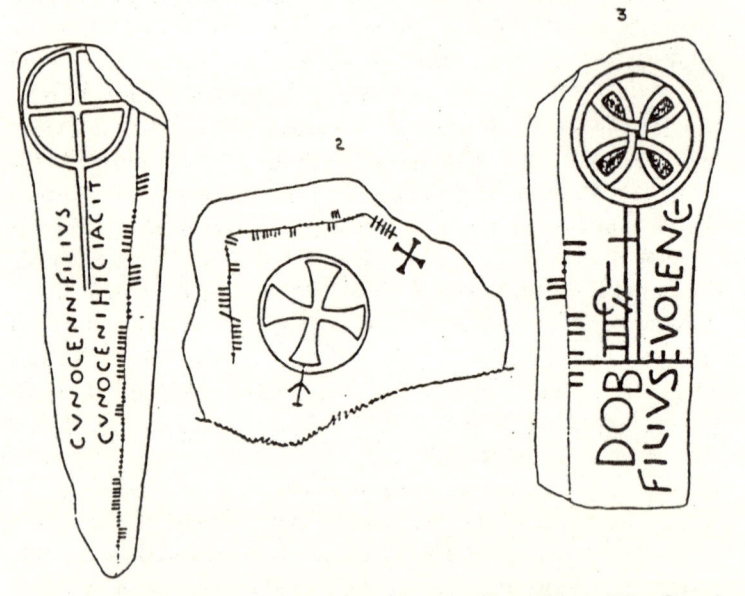

Fig. 10. — Circular Crosses on Stones (1) at Trallong, (2) at Maumenorig, and (3) at Dugoed.

and church bells[7]; but it was never a common Christian symbol. The origin and meaning of the pagan Swastica[8] is beyond the

[1] Northcote and Brownlow's *Roma Sotterranea*, vol. i, p. 206.
[2] *Ibid.*, vol. ii, p. 177.   [3] Stuart's *Sculptured Stones*.
[4] *Proc. Soc. Ant. Scot.*, vol. xv, p. 251.
[5] *Proc. R. I. A.*, vol. xxvii, p. 43; *Journ. R. H. and A. A. of Ireland*, 1880, p. 376.
[6] Waller's *Monumental Brasses*.
[7] *Reliquary*, vol. xxii, pl. 6.
[8] For origin of Swastica, see *Numismatic Chronicle*, vol. xx, p. 18, and Schliemann's *Troy*. The Swastica occurs on a metal circlet with inter-

CELTIC SEPULCHRAL MONUMENTS. 97

scope of our subject; by the Christians it was used merely as a particular form of the cross.

The Maltese cross enclosed within a circle, although one of the oldest forms, has survived in the crosses used for dedicating churches, and in the ones used over Norman doorways. In both these cases it is probable that at some time the Maltese cross has taken the place of the earlier monogram, which exists on the dedication-stone at Jarrow, and was also placed over doorways in Syria, in the sixth century.

The Maltese cross without the circle occurs on three Ogham stones in Ireland;[1] and one pillar with a debased Latin inscription in Glamorganshire.[2]

There are three instances of an incised circle with two cross-lines being carved on Ogham stones,[3] and seven which have perfectly plain crosses, consisting of two lines cutting at right angles.[4] The tau cross appears on a pillar with a debased Latin inscription at Fowey, in Cornwall.[5] This is a very rare instance, although there is another amongst the inscriptions in the Catacombs with the Alpha and

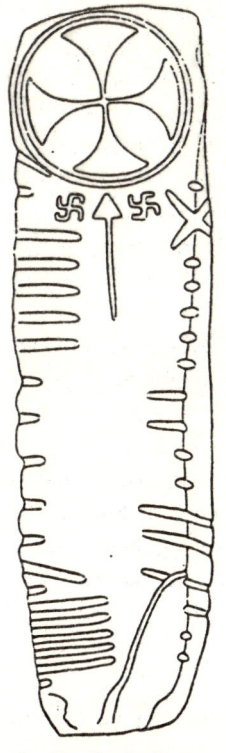

Fig. 11.—Circular Cross on Stone at Aglish. Kerry

laced work, found in Westmoreland (*Journ. B. A. Inst.*, vol. iv, p. 63), and on the capital of a Norman pillar in Essex (*Essex Arch. Soc. Trans.*, vol. ii, New Series, p. 377).

[1] Knockourane, co. Cork, and Maumenorig and Brandon Mountain, co. Kerry. (*Brash*, pls. 14, 21, 27.)

[2] Mynydd Margam. (*Westwood*, pl. 13.)

[3] Drumconwell, co. Armagh (*Journ. R. H. and A. A. of Ireland*); Llanwinio, Caermarthenshire; and Trallong, Brecknockshire. (*Westwood*, pls. 36 and 47.)

[4] Innisvicillane, Trabeg, Ballinahunt, Barrymorereagh, Killeenadreenagh, and Keelogran, co. Kerry (*Brash*, pls. 16, 24, 25, 33, and 34); Caldy Island, Pembrokeshire (*Westwood*, pl. 52). Also on stones with Latin inscriptions at St. Nicholas, Pembrokeshire; Trawsmawr, Caermarthenshire; Fowey, Trigg Minor, and Nanteglos, Cornwall (*Hübner*).

[5] *Journ. B. A. Inst.*, vol. iv, p. 307.

H

Omega.[1] The inscribed pillar at St. Clement's, Truro, has the top formed into a circle with a cross upon it.[2]

There are a few other miscellaneous forms of crosses on rude pillar-stones. At Gowran, co. Kilkenny, and Drumkeare, co. Kerry, the cross has arms, each terminating in a square; at Kinnaird East, co. Kerry, the cross resembles a window-frame, and consists of a square divided into quarters by two cross-lines, the two upper quarters being again subdivided in a similar manner; at Ballintaggart, and Ballintarmon, co. Kerry, the crosses are formed of incised lines[3]; and at Staynton and Bridell, in Pembrokeshire,[4] the crosses are circular.

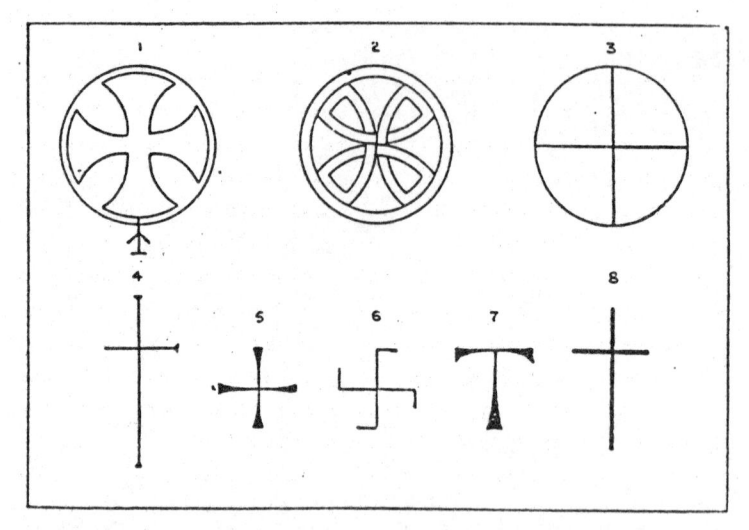

Fig. 12.— Various forms of Crosses on rude Pillar-Stones with Inscriptions.

It only remains now to refer briefly to the rude pillar-stones having crosses but no inscriptions. The age of such monuments can only be guessed at; but when the cross is incised and of simple form, and when the stone on which it is carved is associated with inscribed monuments of undoubted antiquity,

---

[1] De Rossi, *Christ. Inscr. of Rome*, No. 218.
[2] *Journ. B. A. Inst.*, vol. iv, p. 309.
[3] Brash, pls. 28, 39, 25, 22, and 23.
[4] *Archæologia Cambrensis*, and *Westwood*, pl. 54.

CELTIC SEPULCHRAL MONUMENTS. 99

as in the case of the stone at Trawsmawr[1] in Caermarthenshire, or when it is found on an ancient ecclesiastical site now deserted, as in the case of St. Patrick's Chair, near Marown, in the Isle of Man, it may not be unreasonable to ascribe an early date. The cross at Trawsmawr consists of two incised grooves, terminating in round holes or dots, and with four round holes in the angles of the cross. It is carved upon a rude monolith standing erect near a similar stone, with a debased Latin inscrip-

Fig. 13.—Cross on rude Pillar-Stone at Trawsmawr.

tion. St. Patrick's Chair is a small heap of stones, on the top of which are two upright slabs having incised crosses, just like the one at Trawsmawr, but without the four dots in the angles. A very similar cross exists on the stone in the burying ground at Eilean na Naimh,[2] in Scotland, described in a previous course of Rhind Lectures by Dr. Anderson. Another early form of cross found on this class of monument is at Laggangan in Wig-

[1] *Westwood*, pl. 49.
[2] *Scotland in Early Christian Times.*

tonshire,[1] and is of the Latin shape, made in outline with an incised groove, but incomplete at the bottom, where it is left open (fig. 14, No. 3). In each of the four corners are little crosses, taking the place of the dots on the Trawsmawr stone. This reduplication of crosses is also found on a stone at Llanfihangel ar Arth in Caermarthenshire[2] (fig. 14, No. 2), and at a later period on a cross ornamented with interlaced work, at Kilmartin in Argyleshire.[3] It is possible that the five crosses thus produced, or the five round bosses on some of the Celtic ornamental crosses, may have a symbolical significance as referring to our Lord's five wounds.

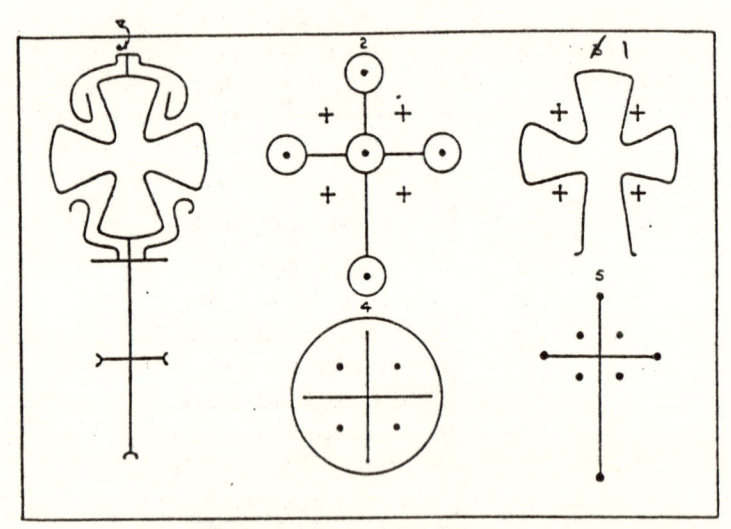

Fig. 14.—Various forms of incised Crosses on rude Pillar-Stones without inscriptions.

We have now concluded our survey of the earliest known Christian monuments in this country, and have shown that although there exists no means by which the exact date of their erection can be determined, yet the period to which they belong has pretty clearly defined limits. On the one hand, Christian symbols which had their origin in another geographical area, cannot be expected to appear in a place at a remote distance

---

[1] *Scotland in Early Christian Times*, 2nd Series, p. 89.
[2] *Westwood*, pl. 48.
[3] *Scotland in Early Christian Times*, 2nd Series, p. 128.

from the centre where they were first invented, until a sufficient time has elapsed to allow of their gradual diffusion through the intervening countries. Thus it would be unreasonable to assume that the cross was introduced into Britain before it found its way into Gaul, or that it was used in Gaul before it was known in Rome. Again, on the other hand, the limit of duration of the earliest types of Christian monuments in Britain is fixed, because their place is taken at a later period by an entirely new class, whose age is determined by historical evidence. The period confined between these two limits extends approximately from A.D. 400 to 700.

We shall now proceed to examine the ornamented sculptured stones which superseded the rude inscribed pillars in the seventh or eighth centuries, and continued in use until the time of the Norman Conquest in A.D. 1066.

The five chief points, already mentioned, in which the earlier Celtic Christian monuments differ from the later ones are: (1) the dressing of the stone; (2) the practice of incising the design instead of sculpturing it in relief; (3) the use of peculiar geometrical and other forms of ornament; (4) the alteration in the letters of the inscriptions; and (5) the introduction of new formulæ in the epitaphs.

As regards the dressing of the stone, the same changes seem to have taken place in the sepulchral monuments as is to be observed in the ecclesiastical buildings; for the early oratories of Ireland, built of uncemented stones put together without the use of the hammer or chisel, and the rude pillars erected to the memory of the Christians who worshipped in them, are nothing more than blocks of slate granite or sandstone in their natural state, untouched by the tool of the mason, except for the cutting of the inscription. Side by side with improvement in the art of building, we find an increased amount of thought and labour expended in the preparation of the memorials of the dead. At the same time that the mason began to square his stones carefully and set them in mortar, the sculptor commenced to reproduce in a harder material the beautiful forms of ornamentation which the Celtic scribes lavished upon the early MSS. of the Gospels. As the art of writing became more common, the shape of the letters altered, and in place of the debased provincial

Latin capitals, which occur universally on the rude pillar-stones, the neater and more rounded minuscule or small letters of the MSS. were introduced for lapidary inscriptions, together with the peculiar Irish letters, ⅄, ʒ, and ſ.[1] In those areas where Scandinavian influence was strong, as in the Isle of Man and parts of Yorkshire and Scotland, the Northern Runic alphabet was used. The angular Latin capitals, with the S formed like a Z and the diamond-shaped O, such as occur in the Saxon and Irish MSS., are also found on inscriptions on stone in England.

The inscriptions on the crosses are carved in horizontal lines across the stone, instead of reading vertically, as on the rude pillar-stones, and are often enclosed in a neat marginal line, so as to form a rectangular panel.

Instead of the "*Hic jacet*" formula of the rude pillar-stones, the later sepulchral slabs in Ireland have "*Oroit do*"[2] ("a prayer for", or "pray for") A. the son of B.; on the crosses of Wales, A. "*preparavit*", or "*fecit, hanc crucem pro anima ejus*", is not uncommon[3]; in the Isle of Man, A. "*raisti crus*" ("raised this cross") "*aft*" ("to the memory") of B. the son of C., is generally found[4]; and on some crosses in England, "*Gibidad der saule*" ("pray for his soul") occurs.[5]

Having now pointed out the chief peculiarities by means of which the rude pillar-stones may be distinguished from the later ornamental sculptured crosses, we shall proceed to examine the symbolism of the latter; but there are first an intermediate class which deserve some passing notice. These are monuments which, although having inscriptions in the minuscule form of letter, are yet almost destitute of dressing and ornamental features. Perhaps the most typical example of the class is the pillar at Killnasaggart, co. Armagh, Ireland. "The name Cell-na-Sagart signifies the Church of the Priests (*Cella Sacerdotum*); but no remains of any church can now be found. There is a small enclosure on a mound, where some traces of ancient sepulture may still be

---

[1] Petrie's *Irish Christian Inscr.*, vol. ii, p. 135.   [2] *Ibid.*, p. 146.
[3] Westwood's *Lapidarium Walliæ*.
[4] J. G. Cumming's *Runic Remains of the Isle of Man*.
[5] Stephens' *Runic Monuments*.

CELTIC SEPULCHRAL MONUMENTS. 103

seen, within which stands a pillar of unmistakable antiquity, on which the following inscription is carved:

Fig. 15.—Pillar-Stone with minuscule inscription at Kilnasaggart.

  IN LOC SO TANIMMAIRNI
  TERNOHC MACCERAN
  BIC ER CUL PETER APSTEL."[1]

(" This place, Ternóc, son of Ciarán the Little, bequeathed it

[1] Petrie's *Irish Inscr.*, vol. ii, p. 27, and pl. 19.

under the protection of Apostle Peter.") The death of Ternoc, son of Ciaran, is recorded in the *Annals of Tighernach*, under the year A.D. 716, and in the *Annals of the Four Masters*, under the year A.D. 714. The possible date of the erection of the monument is therefore fixed by historical data at the beginning of the eighth century; but Miss Stokes expresses some doubt as to its being so old.[1] The inscription is in rounded Irish minuscules, and the language is Irish. The stone stands 7 ft. 4 ins. out of the ground, and measures 1 ft. 6 ins. wide by 6 ins. thick. On the inscribed face are two incised crosses, the upper one of the plain Latin form, and the one at the base having its ends curved round in little spirals, and being enclosed within a circle. On the back of the stone are ten similar crosses within circles, which are, however, in relief, instead of being incised. The pillar is not dressed into shape, but has tool-marks upon it. The dedication to the Apostle Peter recalls the inscription on the Whithorne stone, already described. The cross within the circle is also common to both, and points to an early date.

There are two pillar-stones in the county of Kerry, in Ireland, inscribed in minuscules, and having Maltese crosses within circles and spiral forms of ornament below, all incised. One of these stones is at Kilfountain, and stands near the foundations of an old church in a burial-ground reserved for unbaptised children and suicides. It is inscribed with the founder's name, "FINTEN", and has some Ogham characters upon it which have not been deciphered.[2] The other stone is in the burial-ground of Reask, and has the letters "$\overline{\text{DNE}}$", the contraction for "DOMINE", upon it.[3]

The abbreviations, $\overline{\text{DNS}}$ — $\overline{\text{DNI}}$ — $\overline{\text{DNO}}$, for DOMINUS — DOMINI — DOMINO, are almost unknown except in the county of Kerry,[4] but there is what appears to be a similar inscription upon a stone with a cross found at Papa Stronsay in Orkney.[5]

A rude pillar standing near the doorway of the Church of Kilmalkedar, co. Kerry, has a complete minuscule alphabet cut

---

[1] Petrie's *Irish Inscr.*, vol. ii, p. 29.
[2] *Ibid.*, pl. 3.   [3] *Ibid.*, pl. 4.
[4] *Ibid.*, vol. ii, Nos. 6, 8, 9.
[5] Stuart's *Sculptured Stones*, vol. i, pl. 47.

upon it, together with the contraction DNI and a cross.¹ There are two other rude monoliths with minuscule inscriptions in Ireland; one near the oratory of Gallarus, co. Kerry,² and the other on Inchagoile Island, Lough Corrib, co. Galway.³

There are about ten instances in Wales of stones with minuscule inscriptions and crosses, the most remarkable being the pillar of St. Cadfan, at Towyn in Merionethshire,⁴ which is 7 ft. high and 10 inches wide, the language of the inscription being a very ancient form of Welsh. There are two plain incised crosses upon it. The tall, slender monolith in the churchyard at

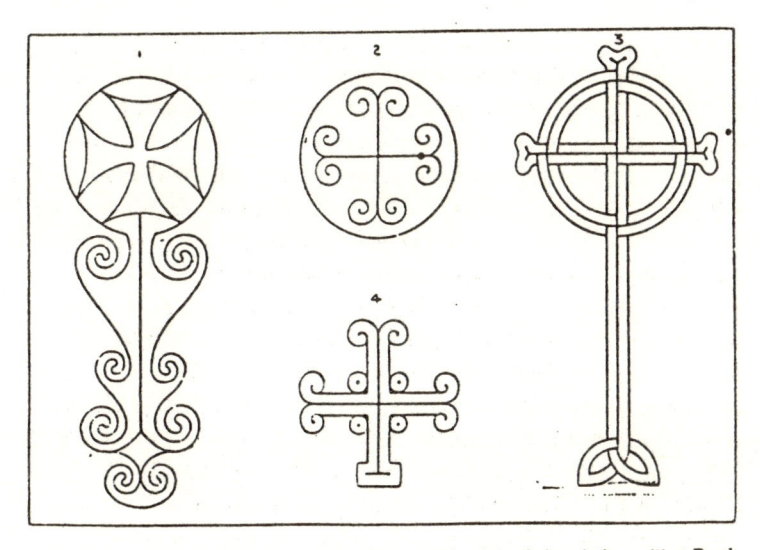

Fig. 16.—Various forms of Crosses on Pillar-Stones with miniscule inscriptions—(1) at Reask, (2) at Kilnasaggart, (3) at Llanwnnws, and (4) at Papa Stronsay.

Llandewi Brefi, in Cardiganshire,⁵ belongs to the same class, and is interesting from its traditional association with St. David, who is supposed to have leaned upon it when preaching at the Synod held at that place in the year A.D. 519, for the suppression of the Pelagian heresy.

[1] Petrie's *Irish Inscr.*, vol. ii, No. 9.
[2] *Ibid.*, vol. ii, No. 10.
[3] *Ibid.*, vol. ii, No. 11.
[4] Westwood's *Lapidarium Walliæ*, pl. 75.
[5] *Ibid.*, pl. 69, No. 2.

### Early Cross-Slabs (A.D. 650-1066).

Passing now from the transitional class of monuments which have just been described, we will turn our attention to the ornamental sculptured stones of the pre-Norman period, all of which are sepulchral, with the exception of some of the more important high crosses. These memorials to the dead are of four kinds: (1) cross-slabs laid horizontally over the grave of the deceased; (2) coped or hog-backed tombstones, also horizontal; (3) erect crosses; (4) small erect head-stones. Each of these will be described in their proper order.

Beginning then with cross-slabs, we find by far the largest and most interesting collection at Clonmacnois, in Ireland, which is situated on the eastern bank of the River Shannon, and was in early times the most important seat of learning in the country. It was founded by St. Ciaran, about the year A.D. 554, and "the value set on this spot as a place of burial arose out of a belief in the power which the patron saint's intercession would have with the Deity on the last day."[1] The remains which exist at the present day at Clonmacnois consist of eight ecclesiastical structures —two round towers, an ancient castle, two magnificent free-standing crosses,[2] to be described hereafter, and about 180 sepulchral slabs, with which we are at present concerned. The value of the information obtained from this source on the early Christian symbolism, palæography, language, and ornamental art cannot be over-estimated, as out of 180 inscribed cross-slabs 81 have been identified, by means of the names recorded, as being the tombstones of bishops, abbots, priests, scribes, kings, lords, and chieftains, the years of whose deaths are mentioned in historical documents such as the *Annals of the Four Masters*, the *Chronicon Scotorum*, and other authorities. We have thus, between A.D. 628 and 1278, a regular series of dated inscriptions, spread over the different centuries in the following proportions:—

---

[1] Petrie's *Irish Inscr.*, vol. i, p. 4.
[2] See Petrie's and Lord Dunraven's works, *On Irish Ecclesiastical Architecture*.

| | | | | | | |
|---|---|---|---|---|---|---|
| 7th century | - | - | - | - | - | 4 |
| 8th " | - | - | - | - | - | 6 |
| 9th " | - | - | - | - | - | 28 |
| 10th " | - | - | - | - | - | 18 |
| 11th " | - | - | - | - | - | 18 |
| 12th " | - | - | - | - | - | 6 |
| 13th " | - | - | - | - | - | 1 |
| | Total | - | - | - | - | 81 |

The method of obtaining a complete chronological series is first to arrange and classify the inscriptions according to the variations in the forms of the letters, the grammatical and declensional peculiarities of the language, and the formulæ of the epitaphs; the changes in the shapes of the crosses used at different times, and the quality of the art exhibited in the ornamental features being also taken into account. The dated inscriptions will then serve as landmarks for ascertaining the age of the undated ones, by merely placing the series arranged in groups archæologically side by side with the historical series arranged in chronological order. Finally, a certain amount of rectification will be necessary so as to render the whole consistent; that is to say, where unimpeachable historical evidence throws doubt upon the arrangement according to the archæological and artistic features, a revision must take place, and *vice versâ*.

These are the principles which guided De Rossi in dealing with the inscriptions of Rome, and Le Blant with those of Gaul.

There are no sepulchral slabs at Clonmacnois which can on historical or other evidence be attributed to the first 84 years after the foundation of the monastery by St. Ciaran (A.D. 544), so that the monuments belonging to this period have either disappeared or present no peculiarities by which they may be identified.

All the slabs at Clonmacnois are inscribed in Irish minuscules, and the only Christian symbol seen is the cross in different forms. They are sculptured on one side only, and were therefore probably intended to lie flat over the grave. An early

Irish poem, preserved in a MS. in the Bodleian Library at Oxford, commences as follows:—

> "Ciaran's city is Cluain-mic-Nois,
> A place dew-bright, red rosed;
> A race of chiefs whose fame is lasting,
> Are hosts under the peaceful clear-streamed place.

> "Nobles of the children of Conn
> Are under the flaggy, brown-sloped cemetery,
> A knot, or an ogham over each body,
> And a fair, just ogham name."[1]

Of the Ogham inscriptions mentioned in this poem only one is known to have existed, and it is now unfortunately lost. It was upon the tombstone of Colman,[2] possibly the Abbot of Clonmacnois of that name whose death is recorded in *Chronicon Scotorum*, A.D. 661. The name Colman, in minuscules, is preceded by a small, plain, incised cross, and below is carved the word "bocht", or poor, in Ogham letters, not on the angle of the stone, but on a stem line, as at Lunnasting and other places in Scotland. There is one other slab at Clonmacnois earlier than that of Colman, and which forms the starting-point of the series of dated stones. It is inscribed in Irish minuscules—

OR DO CHOLUMBON

("Pray for Columban"); and from the earlier character of some of the letters, such as the diamond-shaped O, it may possibly be the epitaph of Columban, Abbot of Clonmacnois, who died A.D. 628.[3]

### *Various forms of Crosses.*

The cross on this slab, which is drawn in outline and destitute of ornament, consists of a central circle connected with four semicircles, whose flat sides face outwards, by bands narrower in width than the diameters of the circle (fig. 17, No. 3). In this particular instance the four arms of the cross are of equal length; but the same shape, with the shaft prolonged, is the one which occurs oftener than any other at Clonmacnois, and may be taken as the one most typically characteristic of the locality. Its use extends from A.D. 887 to 1106, during which period there are

---

[1] Petrie's *Irish Inscr.*, vol. i, p. 5.
[2] *Ibid.*, pl. 2, No. 4.   [3] *Ibid.*, vol. i, pl. 1, No. 3.

CELTIC SEPULCHRAL MONUMENTS.   109

about twenty dated examples, all except one being ornamented with key-patterns, spirals, or interlaced work. The earliest and most beautifully decorated cross of this class is on the tombstone of Suibine Mac Maelhumai.[1] The monument in question possesses a double interest as being one of the most important landmarks in the history of Celtic art in sculptured stonework, and as commemorating a scholar whose fame was so great that his death was considered an event of sufficient importance to be recorded, not only by all the annalists of Ireland, but by the chroniclers of England also. Thus we read in the *Annales*

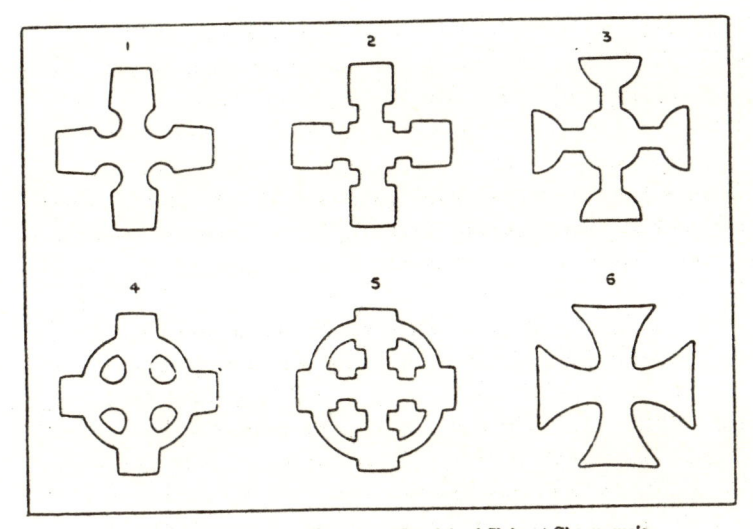

Fig. 17.—Various forms of Crosses on Sepulchral Slabs at Clonmacnois.

*Cambriæ*, under the year A.D. 889: "Subin Scotorum sapientissimus obiit"; and similar testimony to his learning and celebrity is borne by the *Saxon Chronicle*, Florence of Worcester, the *Annals of Ulster*, and the *Chronicon Scotorum*. The identification is rendered complete by the name of the father of Suibine being given in his epitaph, and by the entry in the *Annals of the Four Masters*, under the year A.D. 887,—"Suibhne, son of Maelhumha, anchorite and scribe of Cluain-mic-Nois, died." The name Suibine is equivalent to the modern Sweeney.

[1] Petrie's *Irish Inscr.*, pl. 31, No. 82.

Another fine cross, of a similar shape, ornamented with key-patterns, is on the tombstone of Conaing,[1] son of Congal, Lord of Teffia, who died A.D. 821. There is thus clear evidence that this form of cross was in use as early as the beginning of the ninth century, and also that Celtic ornament was applied to decorative stonework at this period, there being no proof forthcoming that it was used, except in MSS., at an earlier date.

The next most common form of cross found at Clonmacnois to the preceding is one of which there are several variations, as shown on the accompanying diagram (fig. 18), and which in its

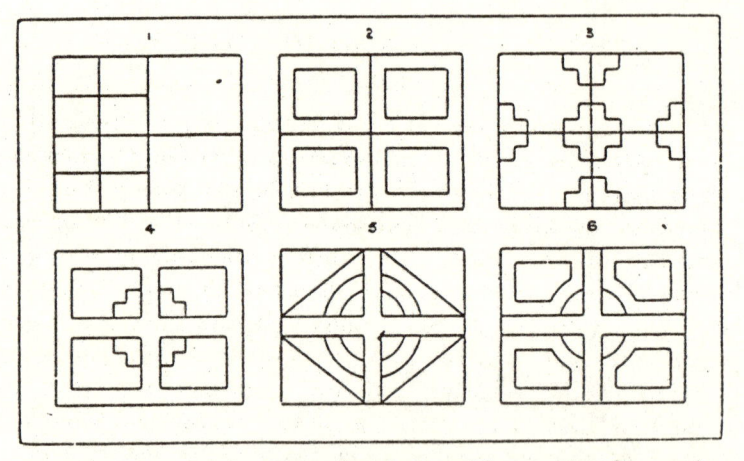

Fig. 18.—Variations of the "Window Frame" pattern of Cross on slabs at Clonmacnois.

simplest shape consists of a rectangle divided into four quarters by two straight lines cutting at right angles, somewhat resembling the panes in a window-frame. The idea, which is that of a cross within a square border, may have been suggested by the covers of the copies of the Gospels. The effect obtained is that of a geometrical pattern, rather than of a cross, the simple beauty of the symbol of our faith being entirely destroyed by the enclosing margin. There are altogether about thirty slabs at Clonmacnois having this type of cross, seven of which have been dated between A.D. 783 and 926. It appears, therefore, that it was

[1] *Petrie*, vol. i, pl. 38, No. 98.

amongst the earliest kinds used, but was gradually superseded by the one first described. Out of the thirty crosses of the window-frame pattern three alone are ornamented, having a Greek fret round the border. The only one of these which has been dated is on the tomb of Tuathgal,[1] Abbot of Clonmacnois, who died A.D. 806.

The most typically Celtic form of cross is derived from the plain Latin cross by surrounding it with a circular ring connecting the arms, and making four circular hollows at the corners where the arms intersect (fig. 17, No. 4). It occurs upon about twenty-two of the slabs at Clonmacnois, six of which are dated between, perhaps, A.D. 651 and 895. Only one shows any trace of ornament, having a pointed end filled in with a little three-cornered triquetra knot.[2] The absence of ornament, and the age of the dated examples, tend to show that this was one of the earliest forms of the cross after the ones enclosed in circles found on the rude pillar-stones, from which it was probably developed by extending the arms beyond the circle. It is to be found on an inscribed slab at Iona,[3] and on a small stone at St. Edrens, in Pembrokeshire.[4]

The next shape of cross to be described consists of a central square, surrounded by four other squares, which are joined together by four bands of narrower width than that of the side of the square (fig. 17, No. 5). A circular ring connects the arms. It occurs upon about seventeen slabs at Clonmacnois, of which eight are dated between A.D. 814 and 889. Except in one instance, which is the earliest (A.D. 889) example of interlaced work here,[5] the cross itself is plain, but in two cases it is enclosed in a rectangular frame of key-pattern, and in others the foot is finished off either with two volute curves,[6] or with a triangular point[7] and a triquetra knot. The form of cross just described is found frequently on the more important erect

---

[1] Petrie's *Irish Inscr.*, vol. i, pl. 12, No. 29.
[2] *Ibid.*, pl. 5, No. 14.
[3] Stuart's *Sculptured Stones*, vol. ii, pl. 65.
[4] *Archæologia Cambrensis*, vol. for 1883, p. 262.
[5] *Petrie*, vol. i, pl. 35, No. 91.
[6] *Ibid.*, vol. i, pl. 18, No. 47.
[7] *Ibid.*, pl. 34, No. 89.

monuments in Scotland and Wales, and also on early sepulchral slabs in England.[1]

Before leaving Clonmacnois two of the less common kinds of crosses must be mentioned. The first occurs on the tombstone of Daniel,[2] and is composed of a double band, forming knots at the extremities of the arms, and passing through a circular ring in the centre. It is, in fact, a cross composed entirely of interlaced work, without any surrounding margin (fig. 19, No. 1).

The other type of cross referred to is that enclosed within a circle, but instead of being plain, as on the early pillar-stones, it

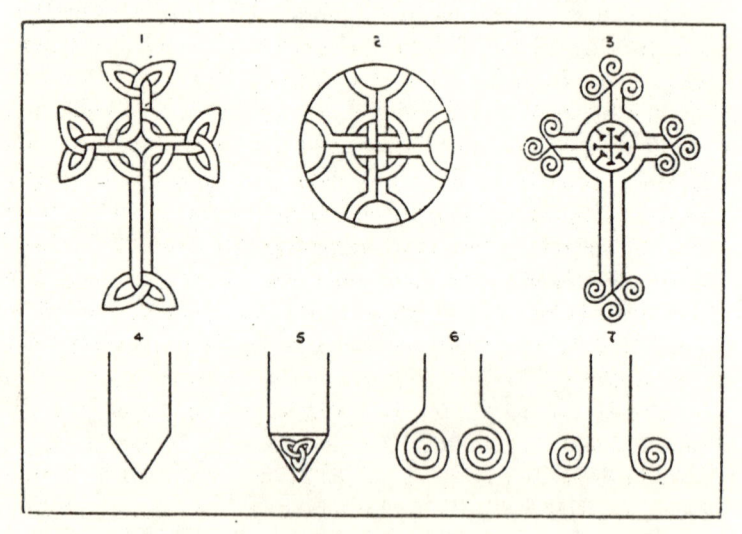

Fig. 19.—Various ornamental forms of Crosses and terminations of arms on slabs at Clonmacnois.

is highly ornamented with key-patterns and interlaced work (fig. 19, No. 2). Three instances exist at Clonmacnois, the most elaborate being on the tombstone of St. Fiachra,[3] who died in

---

[1] On slabs in England, at Monkwearmouth, Hartlepool, Kirkdale; on crosses in Wales, at Llantwit Major, Margam Llanarthney; on slab at Abercrombie in Fifeshire; on cross at Edderton, and about sixteen others in Scotland. (See Stuart's *Sculptured Stones*.)

[2] *Petrie*, vol. i, pl. 35, No. 90, and on Scattery Island. (*Ibid*, vol. ii, pl. 18, No. 37.)

[3] *Petrie*, vol. i, pl. 37, No. 95; also pl. 43, No. 109, and pl. 68, No. 104.

A.D. 921; and there are three other similar ones at Pen Arthur,[1] near St. David's in South Wales. The tombstone of St. Fiachra is interesting, both as being a reliable dated example of Celtic art at the beginning of the 10th century, and because the name of the Saint has been perpetuated in the French word *fiacre*.

Of the plain Latin cross drawn in outline there are only four examples on slabs at Clonmacnois, one of which is dated A.D. 884.[2] The simple cross, composed of two incised lines cutting at right angles, is more common, there being sixteen, out of which seven are dated between the years A.D. 664 and 1021.

The various methods of finishing off the ends of the arms of the crosses with triangular points and spiral curves are shown in the accompanying diagram. (Fig. 19, Nos. 4 to 7.)

The foregoing description of the peculiarities of form exhibited by the different crosses on the sepulchral slabs at Clonmacnois may, perhaps, have appeared to be rather lengthy and tedious, but it is only by studying the most minute details that we can hope to extend our very limited knowledge of early Celtic art and symbolism.

We now pass on to those sepulchral slabs in Ireland and elsewhere upon which other Christian symbols are found in addition to the cross, consisting almost exclusively of abbreviations of the sacred name of Christ, and the Alpha and Omega.

### *The* IHC, XPS, *and* XPI *Abbreviations.*

Up to the present the only contraction of our Lord's name which has been noticed is the Chi-Rho monogram, but this only exists upon the very early pillar-stones, and is entirely wanting upon the later and more highly ornamented monuments. In its place we get the three Greek letters $\chi \bar{\rho} s$, written not in capitals but in minuscules, and sometimes with the old form of s made like a c. The $\chi \bar{\rho} s$ is composed of the first two and last letters of the word $X\rho\iota\sigma\tau\acute{o}s$. There are altogether five examples known of its occurrence upon pre-Norman inscribed stones,—two in Ireland and one in Wales. The most interesting of these is perhaps that on the tombstone of St. Berechtir of

---

[1] Westwood's *Lapidarium Walliæ*, pl. 60.
[2] *Petrie*, vol. i, No. 37.

Tullylease,[1] whose death is recorded on the 6th of December, A.D. 839. He is supposed to have been one of the three sons of a Saxon prince who left England after the defeat of Colman, Bishop of Lindisfarne, by Wilfrid of York, at the Synod of Whitby (A.D. 664).

The tombstone in question is still in the church at Tullylease, in the county of Cork, dedicated to St. Berechtir, and is

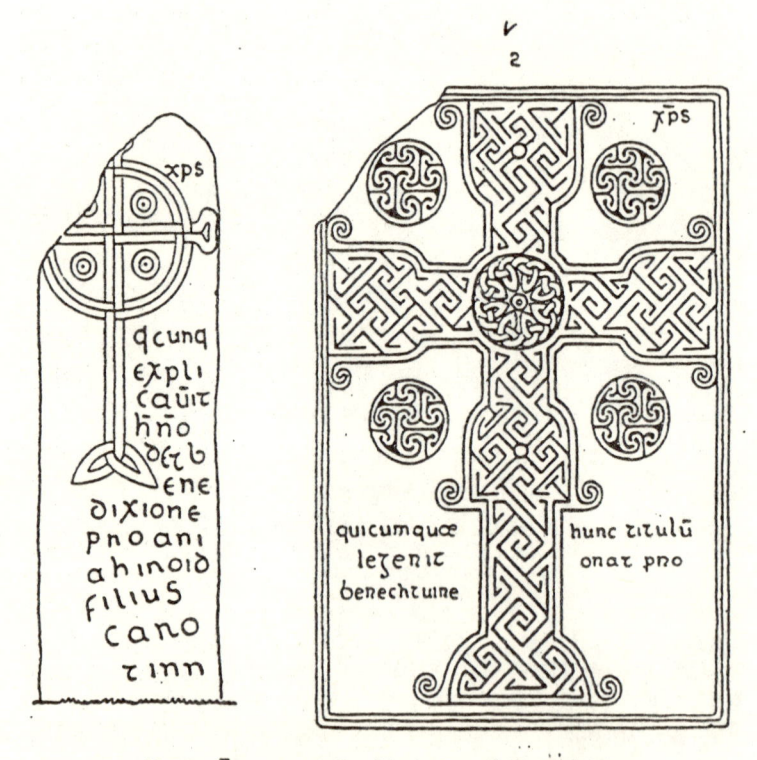

Fig. 20.—X͞PS on stones—(1) at Llan nnwns, and (2) at Tullylease.

one of the most beautiful, and at the same time earliest dated examples of Celtic ornamentation which has survived. The cross upon the slab is covered with a diagonal key-pattern, a central circle is filled in with a wreath of interlaced work, and there are four circles in each of the corners, having spiral devices. The top angle of the stone has been broken away on

[1] *Petrie*, vol. ii, pl. 30.

the left side, where probably the letters I̅H̅S were carved, as on the right the $\overline{\chi\rho\varsigma}$ is still visible. On the lower part of the stone is the following inscription, in Irish minuscules:

>QVICVMQVE HVNC TITVLV̄
>LEGERIT ORAT PRO
>BERECHTVIRE.

("Whoever may read this superscription let him pray for Berechtir.")

Fig. 21.—The Alpha and Omega, I̅H̅S, and $\chi\bar{\rho}s$ on the tombstone of Gurmarc at Pen Arthur.

The stone measures 3 ft. by 2 ft. The $\overline{\chi\rho\varsigma}$, with a somewhat similar formula, is to be seen upon the stone of St. Gwnnws, near Ystrad Meyric Station,[1] in Cardiganshire, which is inscribed as follows in minuscules:

[1] Westwood's *Lapidarium Walliæ*, pl. 68.

QVICVNQVE EXPLICAVERIT HOC NOMEN DET BENEDIXIONEM
PRO ANIMA HIROIDIL FILIVS CAROTINN.

(" Whoever shall have explained this name let him give a benediction for the soul of Hiroidil the son of Carotin."[1])

The two Welsh examples are both in Pembrokeshire; one on a stone from Penarthur, now in St. David's Cathedral, which has a circular ornamental cross, and is inscribed with the name "Gurmarc"[2]; and the other upon a small cross-slab at St. Edrens.[3]

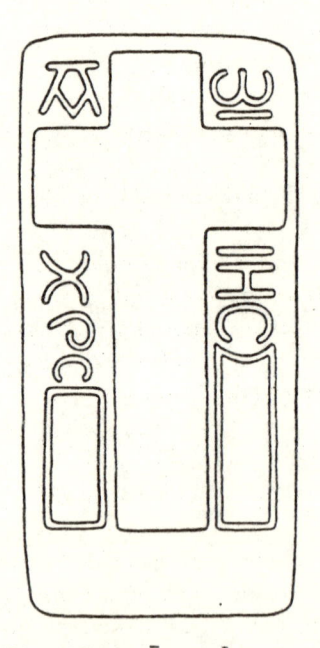

Fig. 22.—The Alpha and Omega, I H̄ C and X̄P̄C, on stone at St. Edrens.

### The Alpha and Omega.

On both the slabs at Penarthur and St. Edrens, besides the X̄P̄C, which has the old form of the Greek s like a c, there is the

[1] This formula appears to have been in use in Ireland in the eighth and ninth centuries; and in the Gospels of MacRegol, in the Bodleian Library at Oxford, there is an entry,—" Quicunque legerit et intellegerit istam narrationem orat pro Macreguil Scriptori."

[2] *Westwood*, pl. 60.

[3] *Archæologia Cambrensis*, vol. for 1883, p. 262.

CELTIC SEPULCHRAL MONUMENTS.       117

Alpha and Omega and the I̅H̅C. The symbolic meaning of the Alpha and Omega is explained by the text in the Revelations (i, 8). The only special feature to be noticed here is, that the line to signify a contraction is placed below the Omega instead of above it. Dr. Reeves considers that the contraction is for the word *et*, between the Alpha and Omega. The Alpha is in the capital form, but the Omega, as is most usual, in the minuscule. The I̅H̅C is an abbreviation of the name IHΣOTC, com-

Fig. 23.—The Alpha and Omega on the tombstone of Hildithryth, at Hartlepool.

posed of the first two and last letters, the old form of the Greek sigma being used.

There is a unique example in Ireland of the Alpha and Omega, the I̅H̅ and the X̅P̅S all occurring together upon the tombstone of "Bresal", now preserved in St. Kevin's Kitchen at Glendalough, in the county of Wicklow.[1] The slab measures 5 ft. 5 ins. long by 2 ft. 3½ ins. broad by 6 ins. thick. The

---

[1] *Journal of the Archæol. Assoc. of Ireland*, vol. vi, Fourth Series (1883), p. 42.

form of the cross is the same as that upon the tombstone of "Daniel", at Clonmacnois (see fig. 19, No. 1), having knots at the extremities of the arms.

Amongst the very interesting series of small inscribed cross-stones found in the years 1833 and 1838, near the site of the Monastery founded by St. Heiu, A.D. 640,[1] and now preserved in the British Museum, are two with the Alpha and Omega, one upon the tombstone of "Hildithryth"[2] (inscribed in Runes), and the other upon the tombstone of "Berchtgyd"[3] (inscribed in semi-uncials). The Alpha is in the capital form, and the Omega made like the letter O, with a vertical stroke through it.

The stones found at Hartlepool, nine in number, although resembling the ordinary cross-slabs in general appearance, differ from them entirely as regards size, as the smallest only measures $7\frac{1}{2}$ ins. by $5\frac{1}{2}$ ins., and the largest about 12 ins. square. The late Rev. D. H. Haigh has identified some of the names commemorated with those of persons living in the seventh and eighth centuries.[4]

An inscribed cross-slab at Billingham, in the county of Durham, bears the Alpha, only the Omega being broken off.[5]

There are only four texts in the Bible mentioning the Alpha and Omega, and these are all to be found in the Apocalypse. There is but one Irish MS. of the New Testament containing the Revelations, namely, the *Book of Armagh*, the date of which is A.D. 807. The passage is thus given in the MS.: "Ego sum Alpha et ω"; the last letter being the Greek minuscule form of Omega, and all the rest written in the ordinary Irish characters.

Greek letters are retained in many of the early Celtic MSS., especially in the contraction $\chi \bar{\rho} \iota$, for Christi, at the beginning of the historical portion of St. Matthew's Gospel, which usually occupies an entire page, magnificently illuminated with the

---

[1] Bede's *Eccl. Hist.*, bk. IV, chap. xxiii.
[2] Hübner's *Christian Inscr.*, No. 189.
[3] *Ibid.*, No. 194.
[4] *Jour. Brit. Archæol. Assoc.*, vol. i, p. 185.
[5] Hübner's *Christian Inscr.*, No. 202.

words "$\overline{\chi\rho\iota}$ autem generatio". This abbreviated form of the Saviour's name in Greek letters occurs upon one of the crosses at Margam, in Glamorganshire,[1] bearing the inscription

CRVX $\overline{\chi\rho\iota}$ ✚ ENNIAVN PRO ANIMA GVOGORET FECIT

("Enniaun made this cross of Christ for the soul of Guogoret");

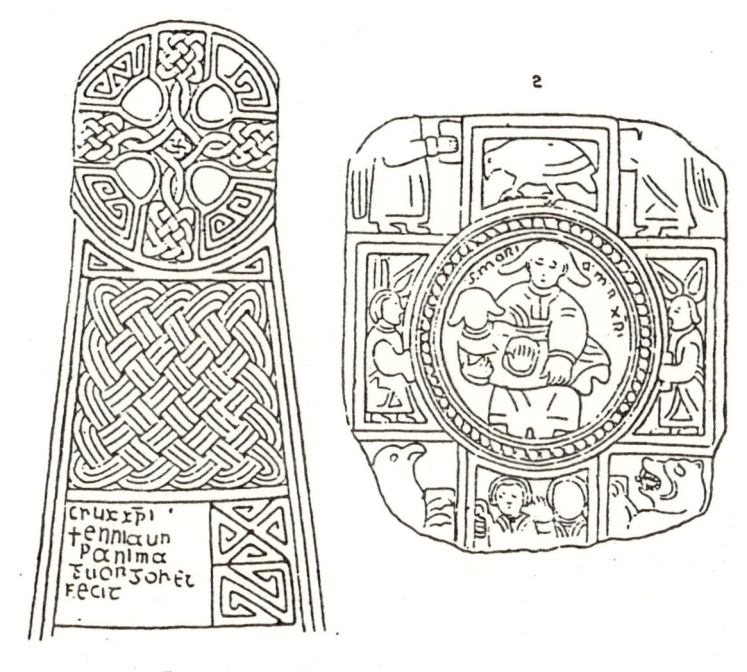

Fig. 24.—The $\overline{\chi\rho\iota}$ abbreviation on sculptured stones—(1) at Margam and (2) at Brechin.

and also upon a sculptured stone at Brechin, in Forfarshire,[2] inscribed

S. MARIA MATER $\overline{\chi\rho\iota}$

("St. Mary, the Mother of Christ.")

The symbolism of the early sepulchral monuments is confined almost exclusively to the cross and monograms expressing the name of Christ; there are, however, a few exceptions.

---

[1] Westwood's *Lap. Walliæ*, pl. 16.
[2] Stuart's *Sculptured Stones*, vol. i, pl. 138.

### The Fish Symbol.

The tombstone of "Oidacan", at Fuerty, in the county of Roscommon, in Ireland, bears a cross, on one side of which is the representation of a fish.[1] The use of the fish as a Christian symbol began in the Catacombs at Rome, where it is found on about a hundred epitaphs, the first dated one belonging to the year A.D. 234. Most of the undated examples may, from various indications, be referred to the first three centuries, and by the

Fig. 25.—Fish symbol on tombstone of Oidacan at Fuerty.

middle of the fourth the fish symbol had become so rare that it is only found on one out of nearly two thousand inscriptions, ornamented with palms, crowns, birds, sheep, and monograms, subsequent to the time of Constantine.[2] "On the Christian inscriptions in Gaul, which generally both begin and abandon the use of each Christian symbol nearly a century later than

[1] Petrie's *Irish Inscr.*, vol. ii, pl. 8, No. 14.
[2] Northcote and Brownlow's *Roma Sotterranea*, vol. ii, p. 58.

they were used or abandoned in Rome, there are only seven examples, either of the word or figure of a fish, among the whole number (exceeding 700) collected and published by Le Blant."[1]

It is found most frequently upon early engraved gems and rings[2] from the Catacombs, and occurs also upon many of the sculptured stones of Scotland and in the Celtic MSS. which will be described hereafter. The use of the fish symbol is continually referred to in the writings of the early fathers, from the time of St. Clement of Alexandria, who, in the second century, recommends the faithful to engrave the figure of a fish upon their seals.[3] The symbol has several meanings, the most universally accepted one being that the fish signifies Christ. The sacred acrostic, in which the first letters of the five Greek words—'Ιησοῦς, Χριστὸς, Θηοῦ, Υἱὸς Σωτήρ ("Jesus Christ, the Son of God : Saviour"), when put together, form the Greek word for fish (ἰχθύς), is well known. Whether the symbol suggested the acrostic, or the acrostic the symbol, can never be decided; but when it was once found out, there is no doubt that the acrostic was the means of making the symbol more popular.

This acrostic is quoted by Eusebius[4] in the fourth century, and St. Augustine[5] in the seventh, from the so-called Sibylline verses,[6] which appear to have been written about the year A.D. 180. The practice of composing sacred acrostics was a common one in all ages of the Church. Thus we read of St. Damasus exercising his ingenuity in writing verses the first letters of which formed the name Jesus[7]; and in later times, the Book of Prayers of Æthelwald, Bishop of Lindisfarne (A.D. 721-740), in the University Library at Cambridge, contains an acrostic dedication in different-coloured inks, forming the name AEDELVALD EPISCOPVS.[8] A double-acrostic is also to be found in the enigmas of Aldhelm, Bishop of Salisbury.

---

[1] Northcote and Brownlow's *Roma Sotterranea*, vol. ii, p. 57 ; and Le Blant, *Inscr. Chrét. de la Gaule*, vol. i, p. 370.

[2] Garrucci, *Storia della Arte Cristiana*, vol. vi, pls. 478-9.

[3] *Pædag.*, iii, 106.

[4] *Oratio Constant. ad Cœt. Sanct.*, § 18.

[5] *De Civit. Dei*, xviii, 25.

[6] Martigny's *Dict.*, pp. 654 and 739.      [7] *Ibid.*, art. "Acrostiche".

[8] Westwood's *Miniatures of Irish MSS.*, p. 45.

When the fish symbol occurs on Christian monuments and objects, it is sometimes accompanied by the Greek word ἰχθύς; but upon an epitaph discovered in 1839, in the ancient cemetery of St. Pierre d'Estrier, near Autun, possibly of the fourth century, the whole of the sacred acrostic is given at full length.[1] De Rossi illustrates a leaden tomb from Saida, in Phœnicia, which bears the Chi-Rho monogram, combined with the word ἸΧΘΤΣ, thus showing clearly the meaning attached to the symbol. In the Catacombs the fish occurs frequently in associa- with the anchor, being then equivalent to "Hope in Christ", or with the dove, to signify "Peace in Christ".

The Scriptural reasons for the adoption of the fish as a Christian symbol are very numerous. The four Apostles, Peter, Andrew, James, and John, were fishermen; and after the miraculous draught of fishes upon the sea of Galilee, our Lord addressed specially to Simon the words, "Fear not; from henceforth thou shalt catch men", upon which he, together with the others, forsook all and followed Him. This scene, although possessing as high a dramatic and religious interest as any incident described in the Gospels, and so familiar to most of us from Raphael's celebrated cartoon, is not amongst the subjects usually found in early Christian art, although it occurs upon an ivory plaque of the eleventh century in the Cathedral of Salerno, in Italy.[2]

The symbolic interpretation which makes the sea to mean the world, the fishes the souls of men, and the ship the Church, was perfectly well understood, as the whole is clearly set forth in the *Livre de Créatures* of Philippe de Thaun,[3] of the twelfth century, which will be more fully described in a future lecture. The omission of the miraculous draught of fishes from the cycle of subjects found in the Catacombs may be accounted for by the fact that the explanation of the fishes to mean the souls of men, clashes with those which either refer to the more important sacramental doctrines, or to Christ Himself. There is, however, one instance of an ivory finial from the Catacombs, representing three men in a boat, one of whom is drawing in a net over the side con-

---

[1] Pitra, *Annales de Philosophie Chrétienne*, vol. xix, p. 195.
[2] Cast in South Kensington Museum, Frame 35 (1874-94).
[3] Thos. Wright's *Treatises on Science during the Middle Ages*, p. 108.

taining a fish.[1] The two miracles of the reduplication of the loaves and the fishes, and Our Lord's feast with the disciples on the shore of the sea of Tiberias after His Resurrection, appear to have given rise to the fish being used as a eucharistic symbol in the early representations of the Last Supper, which will be described subsequently.

St. Melito of Sardis, and also St. Augustine, in commenting on the mystical scene in the last chapter of St. John's Gospel,

Fig. 26.—Tombstone of Donfrid at Wensley.

explain that the fish that was broiled was typical of Christ, who suffered ("the Piscis assus, Christus passus," quoted by Bede).[2]

The fish, as a symbol of the Sacrament of Baptism, has not the warrant of Scripture, but we have testimony that the early Christian Church regarded it as such; for Orientus, writing in A.D. 450, "Piscis natus aquis, auctor baptismatis ipse est";[3] and

[1] Northcote and Brownlow's *Roma Sotterranea*, vol. ii, p. 280.
[2] *Ibid.*, p. 68; Augustine Tract cxxiii, in Johannem xxi.
[3] Martigny's *Dict.*, p. 656.

in Tertullian, *De Baptismo sub init.*, we find, "Nos pisciculi Secundum ἰχθύν Nostrum in aquâ nascimur."[1] Lastly, the miracle of the fish with the tribute money mentioned in St. Matthew, was made a type of Christ offering Himself a sacrifice to pay for the sins of the world; and in the story of the fish caught by Tobias in the Tigris, to deliver Sara from the demon, and to give sight to his father (Tobit, ch. vi), was seen Christ, who conquered the Devil, and was the Light of the World.[2] Similar fish legends are found in the folk-lore of most nations, especially in the East; and the one related of St. Kentigern is illustrated upon the seals of the city of Glasgow.

The cross-slab at Fuerty bearing the fish symbol, the meaning of which has now been fully explained, is quite unique, and the practice of ornamenting this class of sepulchral monument with figure-sculpture was extremely rare. There are, however, a few exceptions, such as the tombstone of "Donfrid", at Wensley, in Yorkshire,[3] which has two birds and two beasts carved in the angles of the cross; an uninscribed slab at Cross Canonby, in Cumberland,[4] has a rude figure of a man at one side of the cross; and another, at Hackthorne in Lincolnshire,[5] has an eagle at each side above, and three-cornered triquetra knots below.

## EARLY ERECT HEADSTONES.

The most common form of early sepulchral monument appears to have been a cross-slab laid horizontally over the grave; but it was also the custom sometimes to place a small erect stone at the head of the grave. These headstones were very much like the ones in use at the present day in churchyards, being rounded at the top and ornamented with a simple cross. Early ones, perhaps belonging to pre-Norman times, have been found at Adel,[6] in Yorkshire, Thurnby,[7] in Leicestershire, Cam-

---

[1] Tyrwhitt's *Art Teaching of the Primitive Church*, p. 339.
[2] Martigny's *Dict.*, p. 654.
[3] *Journ. Brit. Archæol. Assoc.*, vol. vii, p. 75.
[4] *Trans. Cumb. and West. Ant. Soc.*, vol. v, p. 149.
[5] *Journ. Brit. Archæol. Inst.*, vol. v, p. 400.
[6] *Ibid.*, vol. xxvii, p. 77.
[7] *Assoc. Arch. Soc. Rep.*, 1871, p. 183.

bridge,[1] and elsewhere. The most remarkable example, however, is one of the Saxon period at Whitchurch, in Hampshire,[2] with the inscription:

    ✠ HIC CORPVS FRIΘBVRGAE REQVI
      ESCIT IN PACEM SEPVLTVM :·

("Here lies the body of Frithburga, buried in peace.") The stone measures 1 ft. 10 ins. high by 1 ft. wide by 9 ins. thick. The top is semicircular, and the inscription runs round the edge. On the front is carved a bust of Christ, with cruciferous nimbus, holding a book in one hand, and giving the benediction with the other. On the back is an elegant scroll ornament.

Fig. 27.—Inscription round the headstone of Frithburga at Whitchurch. (*From a rubbing by the Rev. G. F. Browne.*)

## HOG-BACKED RECUMBENT MONUMENTS.

The last kind of early sepulchral monument we have to consider in this lecture is the coped or hog-backed tombstone, which is found in Scotland and the north of England, but not in other parts of Great Britain. There exists no means of determining the exact age of any of the coped stones, but the ornamental features correspond in many cases with those of the sculptured crosses of the pre-Norman period. Some of the coped stones still remain *in situ*, showing that they were placed horizontally over the graves of the deceased. The shape of one of these monuments somewhat resembles a boat turned upside down, the average size being about 6 ft. long by 1 ft. 6 ins. high and the same wide. There is generally a central ridge running the whole length of the stone, from which the two sides slope away on each side, like the roof of a house. This ridge is higher in the middle than at the ends, so as to give a hog-backed appearance, and the sloping sides are ornamented

---

[1] *Archæologia*, vol. xxvii, p. 228.
[2] Hübner's *Christian Inscr.*, No. 165.

with scales, either to imitate those of an animal or the tiles of a roof. The most remarkable feature of all is the way in which heads and bodies of grotesque beasts are made to form the two ends. Sometimes the whole stone assumes the shape of a scaly animal, with the head at one end and the four feet carved upon the side, as at Govan, near Glasgow[1]; at another time we find two muzzled bears facing each other, grasping each end of the stone with their paws, as at Brompton, in Yorkshire; but in

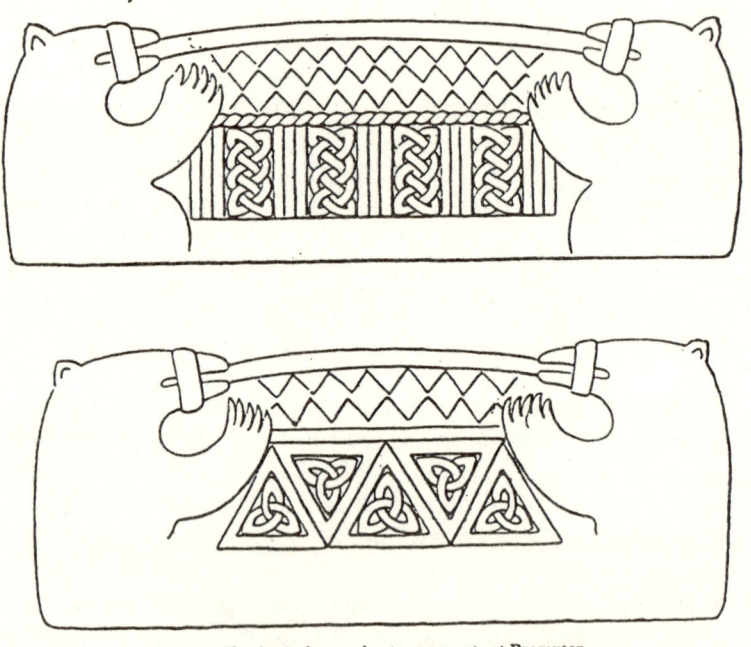

Fig. 28.—Hog-backed recumbent monuments at Brompton.

most cases there is nothing more than a huge head, with eyes and ears at each end, as at Heysham, in Lancashire.[2]

The later coped tombstones are not zoomorphic or hog-backed, but are made more in the shape of the metal shrines of the twelfth century, having the sloping top ornamented with scales and the sides with arcading. This was probably the form of

---

[1] Stuart's *Sculptured Stones*, vol. i, pl. 134.

[2] Cutt's *Sepulchral Slabs* and *Journ. Brit. Archæol. Assoc.*, vol. xlii, p. 341.

the tomb of St. Chad, who died on the 2nd of March, A.D. 672, and was buried at Lichfield; for Bede tells us that "the place of his sepulchre is covered with a wooden monument made like a small dwelling-house, having an opening in the wall, through which those who come for the sake of devotion are wont to put their hand, and take thence some of the dust, which when they have put in water, and given it to sick beasts of burden, or men to drink, the grievance of their infirmity being presently removed, they return to the joys of desired health."[1]

Whether the zoomorphic terminations of the hog-backed stones have any special symbolic meaning, it is impossible to say.

*Man in ancient Attitude of Prayer.*—In some cases the sides of these monuments are ornamented with figure-sculpture, as upon one on the Island of Inchcolm,[2] which has a rudely executed figure of a man with both hands upraised. This is the ancient attitude of prayer, as seen in the representations of the Oranti and Daniel in the Den of Lions, in the paintings in the Catacombs. Figures in this position are not uncommon in Celtic art, and there can be little doubt that they were copied from the early Christian Oranti, and that the meaning of both is the same.

At Lower Heysham, in Lancashire, is a very fine hog-backed stone, 6 ft. 8 ins. long and 2 ft. high, with huge animal heads at each end, and having both sides covered with figure-sculpture. The subject on the front is a hunting scene, with a stag and hounds and four men with hands upraised, as at Inchcolm; upon the back is a stag, a man with his hands upraised, and a tree with three birds. The Christian interpretation of hunting scenes will be discussed in a future lecture, the peculiar feature here being the men in the ancient attitude of prayer.

Of the coped tombstones shaped like a shrine there is a very beautiful specimen, which may possibly belong to the Saxon period, in Peterborough Cathedral. It is 3 ft. 5 ins. long, 1 ft. 2 ins. wide, and 2 ft. 4 ins. high. The two ends are vertical; the sides taper slightly, and the top has two sloping faces like the roof of a house. Each side has arcades, consisting of six

---

[1] Bede's *Eccl. Hist.*, bk. IV, ch. iii.
[2] *Proc. Soc. Ant. Scot.*, vol. xix, p. 406.

compartments, with semicircular arched tops, each enclosing a full-length figure, with the nimbus round the head and carrying a book. In one case the nimbus is cruciferous, so that the figure whose head it adorns is intended for Christ. The others are possibly the Apostles. Each of the sloping faces of the

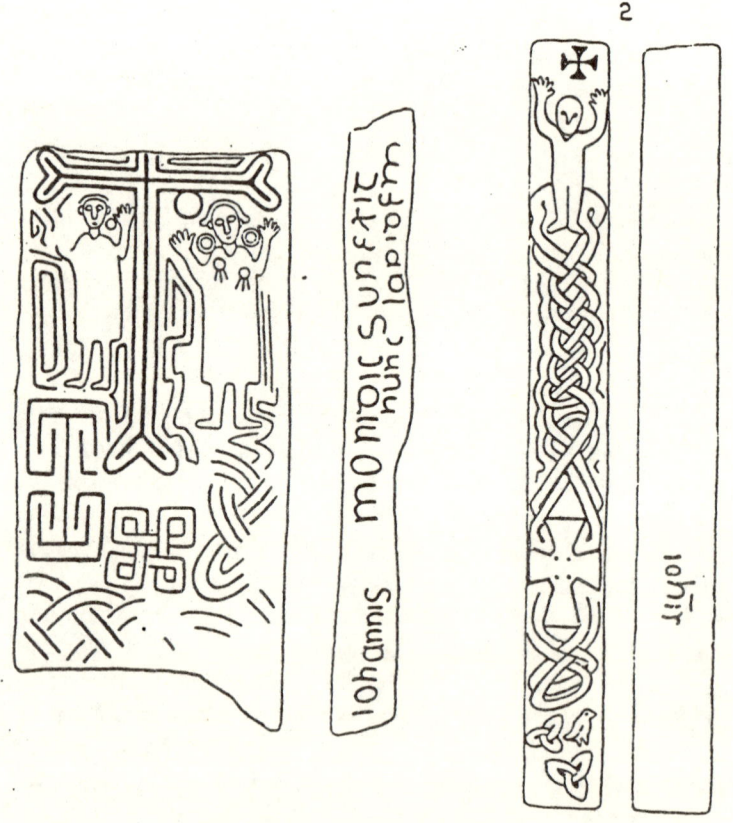

Fig. 29.—Man in ancient attitude of prayer on stones—(1) at Llanhamlkch, Brecknockshire, and (2) at Llanfrynach, in the same county.

top is divided into four panels, ornamented with scrolls of foliage, and birds, dragons, and interlaced work.

Up to the present all the sepulchral monuments we have examined have been those placed as memorials over the graves of the deceased; but there is at least one instance where the sarcophagus containing the body is decorated with symbolic sculptures. The stone coffin referred to was dug up in Govan Churchyard, near Glasgow, in the year 1855.[1] Its interior dimensions are 6 ft. long by 1 ft. 2 ins. to 1 ft. 4 ins. wide by 1 ft. 3 ins. deep, the thickness of the sides and bottom being 5 ins. The two ends are covered with interlaced work, and the two sides are each divided into four panels, filled in alternately

Fig. 30.—Two sides of Stone Coffin at Govan.

with figure-sculpture and interlaced work. The principal subject represented is a hunter on horseback, with a dagger at his side, pursuing a stag. On the flank of the horse is inscribed the letter A. The other subjects are groups of animals.

[1] Stuart's *Sculptured Stones*, vol. i, pls. 34 and 35.

## GENERAL INDEX

Acrostic, 121
Aidan, St., 80
Arcosolia, 12
Art, styles of, 10, 19, 40
Augustine, St., landing of, 71

Bede, Venerable, 71
Belt-clasps, Burgundian, 56
Berechtuire, St., 84
Book-covers, ivory, 62

Cadoc, St., 81
Canute, King, 59
Casket, ivory, 63
Catacombs, 11-26
Celtic, monuments, 77, church, tonsure and keeping of Easter, 78
Chairs, episcopal, 65
Charles the Bald, psalter of, 58
Christianity, first introduced into Great Britain, 71; into Ireland, 79; into Scotland, 80; into Northumbria, 80; into Wales, 81
Chrysostom, St., 71
Ciaran, St., 106
Colman, 108
Columba, St., 80
Columban, 108
Combs, ivory, 64
Crosses, pre-Norman, characteristic of, 83, 101; dated examples of, 84; formulae of inscriptions on, 102
Crucifixes, ivory, 65
Cunigunda, casket of, 59
Cybi, St., 81

Damascus, Pope, 15
Daniel, 112
David, St., 81; at Llandewi Brefi, 105
Dedication stones, 93
Diptychs, ivory, 60
Donfrid, 123
Doors of Churches, 66
Dubricius, St., 80
Egfrid, King, 94

Foacraich, St., 84, 112
Flabella, ivory, 64
Furius Dionysius, almanack of, 14

Galla Placidia, chapel of, 35; coins of, 73
Germanus, St., of Auxerre, 79
Gildas, 71, 81
Gilded glass vessels from the catacombs, 27-32
Gunhilda, cross of, 59
Gregory, St., 51

Headstones, Saxon, 124
Herebert, St., comb of, 64
Hermes Kriophorus, 20
Hilary, St., 79
Howel ap Rhys, cross of, 84

Iltutus, St., 81
Itineraries, for pilgrims to the catacombs, 14
Ivories, 57-65

Jerome, St., 71

Lamps, with Christian subjects, 50
*Liber Pontificalis*, 14
Lupus, St., comb of, 64, 79

Manuscripts, 68
Martin, St., 80
Martyrologies, 14
Maximianus, chair of, 65
Medard, St., 69
Melisenda, 63
Mosaics, 39-49

Ninian, St., 80

Oil vessels, holy, 51-53
Oswald, St., 80

Pastoral staff, ivory, 64
Patrick, St., 79
Paulinus, St., 81
Pavements, Roman, 74, 76
Paxes, ivory, 64
Pelagius, St., 71
Peter, St., monuments dedicated to, 90, 103
Pliny, doves of, 40; Nat. Hist., 21
Psalter, Gallican, 79
Pyxes, ivory, 63

Rambona, diptych of, 62

Samson, St., of Dol, 81
Samson, Cross of, 84
Sarcophagi, sculptured, 32-39, 72, 129
Sepulchral monuments, Celtic, 82-84
Sepulchral slabs at Clonmacnois, 106-108
Sepulchral hog-backed recombant monu-

ments, 125
Suibine, 84, 109
Symbolism 1, 2
Symbols 4-9

Teilo, St., 80
Theodolinda, 51
Triptychs, ivory, 62

Valerius Amandinus, sarcophagus of, 72
Villa, Roman, 77

Water-vessels, holy, 54, 55

## INDEX OF SUBJECTS OCCURRING IN CHRISTIAN ART

*Note:* The numbers marked with an asterisk show the page on which the subject is specially described in detail

Abel, 37, 42, 43
Abraham, and Melchisedec, 42, 43; sacrificing Isaac, 20, 29, 30, 37, 43
Acrostic, symbol, 121
Adam and Eve, creation of, 37, temptation of 20, 29, 31, 32, 37, 55, 69
Agatha, St., 45
Agnes, St., 30, 44
Agnus Dei, performing miracles, 36
Alpha and Omega, 23, 42, 55, 77, 116*
Amphora, 32
Anchor, 22
Angels, supporting aureole, 49
Anne, St., 30
Apollinarius, St. 42
Apostles, 29, 30, 42, 43, 45, 52,
Aureole, 43, 53, 63

Bethlehem and Jerusalem, with sheep issuing from gates of, 30, 41-45

Callistus, St., 30
Candlesticks of Jews, 31; of the Apocalypse, 41
Caps, Phrygian, 53
Cecilia, St., 45
Children, three in fiery furnace 21, 29, 37
Chi-Rho monogram, 23, 55, 75*, 77, 86 various forms of, 91; earliest instance of, 91
Christ, as Orpheus 20; as the Good Shepherd, 25, 37, 51, 54; as a man, 29, 30, 42, 43, 45, 53; Chi-Rho monogram and cross in glory, 44, 45; treading on the asp and basilisk, 51; treading on the serpent, 55; IHC, XPS, and XPI abbreviations of name of, 113*; DNS DNI, DNO abbreviations of title of, 104; seated on globe, 42

----scenes from the life of:- nativity, 38, 52; adoration of the Magi, 21, 38, 42, 52, 53, 59; angel and shepherds, 53; Herod and the Magi, 21; presentation in the temple, 41; baptism of, 38, 43, 52, 55; temptation of, 70; giving keys to St. Peter, 38; and woman of Samaria, 21, 38; transfiguration of, 43; entry into Jerusalem 38

----Miracles of, 44; Cana, 21, 30, 38, 55; healing paralytic 21, 29, 31, 38; haemorissa, 38; blind, 21, 38; raising Lazarus, 21, 24, 29, 31, 32, 38; Jairus's daughter, 38; calming the wind and the sea, 21; draught of fishes, 122; loaves and fishes, 21, 24, 31, 38

----Parable of wise and foolish virgins, 21

----Scenes from the passion of:- betrayal, 38; led away to Caiaphas, 70; denial of St. Peter, 38; apprehension of St. Peter, 38; before Pilate, 38; crowned with thorns, 38; carrying cross, 38

----Crucifixion, 52, 53; resurrection, 52; ascension, 52

Church, as a woman, 23; model of, held by patron saint, 41, 44, 45
Ciprianus, St., 30
Classis, city of, 43
Cosmas, St., 41

Cross, 37; on mosaics, 42, 44; on Roman sarcophagus, 73; on Roman pavements, 76; developed out of Chi-Rho monogram, 94; on inscribed pillar stones, 98; on uninscribed pillar stones, 100; on pillar stones with miniscule inscriptions, 105; on Celtic sepulchral slabs, 109

Damianus, St., 41
Daniel, feeding the dragon, 31, 37; in the lion's den, 21, 31, 32, 37, 55, 56, 58; Habakuk bringing food to, 37, 55, 56; with Habakuk lifted up by the hair of his head, 55
David, King, 62; scenes from the life of, 69; anointed by Samuel, 63; slaying the lion, 63; killing Goliath, 21, 63; playing the harp, 63
Dextera Dei, 23, 37
Dolphin, 22, 39
Doves, 22; pair of, drinking from vase, 35

Ecclesius, 42
Elders, four and twenty of Apocalypse, 45
Evangelists, as men, 42; as rivers of paradise, 30; as symbolic beasts, 41, 43-45

Feasts, 28
Felicianus, Pope, 41
Fish, 22, 30, 120*
Fossor, 23
Fountain, mystic, 69

Gervasius, St., 42
God the Father, as a Man, 37
Grapes, carried by spies, 31, 38, 51; on mosaics, 40

Gregory, St., 62
Heavens, personified, 36
Hippolytus, St., 30, 42
Honorius, Pope, 44
Hunting scenes, 31

Implements, used in trades, 24
Isaiah, prophet, 29, 42

James, St., 46
Jeremiah, prophet, 42
Jerusalem, destruction of, 59
Jews, 30, 42; candlesticks of, 30
John, St., Baptist, decapitation of, 54
Jonah, story of, 21, 24, 31, 32, 37, 51, 58
Jordan, river, 30
Joseph, story of, 58
Judas, 30

Labarum, of Constantine, 75
Laurence, St., 30, 42
Law, rolls of, 31
Libernica, St., 30
Luke, St., 30

Manna, fall of, 38
Marcellanus, St., 28, 30
Marriage, rite of, 31
Mary, St., the blessed virgin, 23, 29, 44; annunciation, 41, 52, 55; salutation, 52
Medallion, circular, 42
Mennas, St., 53, 63
Mercy, acts of, 63
Monogram, of Maximian, 43, of Pope Paschal, 45; see Chi-Rho
Moses, at burning bush, 20, 37, 42; receiving the law, 37l; striking rock, 20,

24, 29, 30, 37; and brazen serpent, 29, 30; as St. Peter striking rock, 30, 32

Nimbus, cruciferous, 53
Noah, in the ark, 20, 24, 37

Olive branch, 22
Oranti, 23, 29, 54, 57, 127*

Palm, branch, 33, 54; tree, 45
Paschal, Pope, 45
Paul, St., apostle, 28, 30, 37, 41, 42, 44
Peacocks, 22; pair of, drinking from vase, 54
Pelagius, St., 42
Peter, St., 21, 30, 37, 41, 42, 44; raising Tabitha, 38
Phoenix, 30, 42, 54
Primus, St., 42
Protasius, St., 44
Quails, fall of, 38

Ravenna, city of, 44
Rebuses, 24
Red sea, passage of, 37
Reparatus, Archbishop, 43
Rod, of power, 31

Saints, 28, 30, 44
Sheep, 22
Ship, 24
Shrine, 126
Simon, St., 30
Sixtus, St., 30
Sol and Luna, 53
Spies, carrying bunch of grapes 31, 38, 51

Stag, 54, 129
Stephen, St., 42; martyrdom of, 38
Susanna and the elders, 22, 32
Swastica, 96
Symmachus, 44

Tau Cross, 97
Theodora, Empress, 42
Theodore, St., 41
Throne, 43
Timothy, St., 30
Tobit, 30

Vase, 54
Venantius, St., 44
Vincent, St., 30
Vine, 54
Vintage scenes, 54
Vitalis, St., 42

Well, 23
Wolf, 22

## INDEX OF PLACES

Aghadoe, 64
Aglish, 95
Alexandria, 53
Amalfi, 66
Arles, 35, 53, 71
Arnex, 56
Augsburg, 66
Autun, 54

Ballinahunt, 97
Ballintaggart, 98
Ballintarmon, 98
Ballymorereagh, 97
Balme, 57
Bari, 67
Battersea, 77
Benvenuto, 67
Berlin, 64
Bewcastle, 85
Blye, 56
Bofflens, 56
Brandon, Mt., 97
Brescia, 58
Bridell, 98
Brunswick, 60
Brussels, 59

Cairo, 67
Caldy Island, 97
Cambridge, 59, 124
Cammin, 59
Canterbury, 79
Catterick Bridge, 77
Chedworth, 77
Cividale, 64
Clonmacnois, 84

Collingham, 85
Cologne, 27, 64, 67
Constantinople, 46, 54
Copenhagen, 59
Corbridge, 77
Craigentarget, 96
Cross Canonby, 124

Dol, 81
Dromconwell, 97
Drumkeare, 98
Dublin, 26
Dugoed, 95

Echallens, 57
Edinburgh, 26
Edrens, St., 116
Eilean-na-Naimh, 99

Florence, 27, 53, 61
Fowey, 97
Frampton, 74
Fuerty, 120

Gallerius' Oratory, 105
Genoels, Elderen, 59
Glendalough, 117
Govan, 126, 129
Gowran, 98

Hackness, 85
Hackthorne, 124
Harpole, 76
Hartlepool, 118
Helen's, St., 86
Hilary, St., 79
Hildesheim, 67

Horkstow, 76

Inchagoile, 105
Innisvicillane, 97

Jarrow, 93
Jerusalem, 53
Just, St., 86

Keelogran, 97
Kilfountain, 104
Killeenadreenagh, 97
Kilmankedar, 104
Kilmartin, 100
Kilnasaggart, 102
Kinnaird, East, 98
Kirk Madrine, 88
Knockourane, 97
Laggangan, 99
Lausanne, 57
Lenton, 53
Liverpool, 26, 55, 60
Llanbleddian, 79
Llancarvan, 81
Llandewi Brefi, 81, 105
Llanfihangel-ar-Arth, 100
Llanfrynach, 128
Llanhamllech, 128
Llantwit Major, 81
Llanwinio, 97
Llanwnnws, 115
London, 26, 27, 53, 60, 72

Macon, 56
Marnens, 57
Marown, 99
Marseilles, 35

Maumenorigh, 95
Miannay, 55
Milan, 35, 55
Mongifi, 56
Monreale, 67
Montdidier, 56
Monte Gargano, 57
Monza, 14, 51, 62
Munich, 59
Murano, 54
Mynydd Margham, 97

Nanteglos, 97
Naples, 27
Newcastle, 26, 77
Newton, 96
Nicholas, St., 97
Novgorod, 67

Paris, 27, 53
Pen Arthur, 113
Penmachno, 88
Peterborough, 127
Phillack, 86
Pisa, 35, 67
Podgoritza, 31

Ravello, 67
Ravenna, 35, 41, 58
Rome, 11, 19, 33, 40, 67, 68
Rufford, 54
Ruthwell, 85

Salisbury, 26
Sandbach, 54
Sempringham, 67
Sens, 64

Sheffield, 26
Silian, 95
Sinai, Mt., 40
Staplehurst, 67
Staynton, 98
Stillingfleet, 67
Sydenham, 54

Thurnby, 124
Towyn, 105
Trallong, 96, 97
Trawsfynydd, 93
Trawsmawr, 97
Tullease, 84, 114
Turin, 53

Verona, 67
Versas, 67
Verulam, 79
Vienna, 68
Vigeans, St., 85
Villecheveux, 57
Villecin, 56

Westminster, 72
Whitby, 78
Whitchurch, 125
Whithorne, 79, 80, 90
Whittenham, Long, 55

York, 26, 77

## LIST OF ILLUSTRATIONS.

Cross at Castle Dermot, co. Kildare . . . *Frontispiece.*
St. George overcoming the Pagans. Sculptured above Doorway of Fordington Church, Dorsetshire . . *Title*

| FIG. | | PAGE |
|---|---|---|
| 1. | Cross on lid of Sarcophagus of Valerius Amandinus . | 73 |
| 2. | The Chi-Rho Monogram from Roman Villas—(1 and 2) at Chedworth and (3) at Frampton . . . | 74 |
| 3. | The Chi-Rho Monogram on Stones in Cornwall—(1) at St. Just, (2) at St. Helen's Chapel, (3) at Phillack . | 86 |
| 4. | Chi-Rho Monogram on Stone at Penmachno . . | 87 |
| 5. | Chi-Rho Monogram on Stones at Kirkmadrine . | 89 |
| 6. | Combined Cross and Monogram on Stone at Whithorne | 90 |
| 7. | Various forms of the Chi-Rho Monogram . . | 91 |
| 8. | Chi-Rho Monogram on Dedication Stone at Jarrow . | 93 |
| 9. | Development of Cross out of Monogram on Stones—(1) at Penmachno, (2) Kirkmadrine, (3) Whithorne, (4) Aglish | 94 |
| 10. | Circular Crosses on Stones—(1) at Trallong, (2) at Maumenorig, and (3) at Dugoed . . . . | 96 |
| 11. | Circular Cross on Stone at Aglish . . | 97 |
| 12. | Various forms of Crosses on rude Pillar-Stones with inscriptions . . . . . | 98 |
| 13. | Cross on rude Pillar-Stone at Trawsmawr . . | 99 |
| 14. | Various forms of incised Crosses on rude Pillar-Stones without inscriptions . | 100 |
| 15. | Pillar-Stone with minuscule inscription at Kilnasaggart . | 103 |
| 16. | Various forms of Crosses on Pillar-Stones with minuscule inscriptions—(1) at Reask, (2) at Kilnasaggart, (3) at Llanwnnws, and (4) at Papa Stronsay . | 105 |
| 17. | Various forms of Crosses on Sepulchral Slabs at Clonmacnois | 109 |
| 18. | Variations of the "Window Frame" pattern of Cross on slabs at Clonmacnois . . . . | 110 |
| 19. | Various ornamental forms of Crosses and terminations of arms on slabs at Clonmacnois . . | 112 |
| 20. | $\overline{XPS}$ on stones—(1) at Llanwnnws, and (2) at Tullylease | 114 |
| 21. | The Alpha and Omega, $I\overline{H}S$, and $\chi\overline{\rho}s$, on the tombstone of Gurmarc at Pen Arthur . . . | 115 |

## LIST OF ILLUSTRATIONS.

22. The Alpha and Omega, I H C, and χ$\bar{\rho}$C, on stone at St. Edrens . 116
23. The Alpha and Omega on the tombstone of Hildithryth, at Hartlepool . . . . . . . 117
24. The χ$^{\rho\iota}$ abbreviation on sculptured stones—(1) at Margam and (2) at Brechin . . . . . . 119
25. Fish symbol on tombstone of Oidacan at Fuerty . . 120
26. Tombstone of Donfrid at Wensley . . . 123
27. Inscription round the headstone of Frithburga at Whitchurch 125
28. Hog-backed recumbent monuments at Brompton . . 126
29. Man in ancient attitude of prayer, on stones—(1) at Llanhamllech, Brecknockshire, and (2) at Llanfrynach, in the same county . . . . . . . 128
30. Two sides of Stone Coffin at Govan . . . 129

In the same series:

THE HIGH CROSSES OF IRELAND
BY J. ROMILLY ALLEN

NORMAN SCULPTURE
AND THE MEDIAEVAL BESTIARIES
BY J. ROMILLY ALLEN

Other Llanerch books include:

SYMBOLISM OF THE CELTIC CROSS
by Derek Bryce

THE CHRONICLE OF
HENRY OF HUNTINGDON
translated by Thomas Forester

THE LIFE OF CEOLFRID
BY AN ANONYMOUS MONK OF JARROW
translated by D. S. Boutflower.

From booksellers.
For a complete list, write to:
Llanerch Publishers, Felinfach,
Lampeter, Dyfed, SA48 8PJ.